Carrhae to Nisibis, 53 BC–AD 217

COMBAT

Roman Soldier

VERSUS

Parthian Warrior

Si Sheppard

Illustrated by Johnny Shumate

OSPREY PUBLISHING
Bloomsbury Publishing Plc

Kemp House, Chawley Park, Cumnor Hill, Oxford OX2 9PH, UK
29 Earlsfort Terrace, Dublin 2, Ireland
1385 Broadway, 5th Floor, New York, NY 10018, USA
Email: info@ospreypublishing.com
www.ospreypublishing.com

OSPREY is a trademark of Osprey Publishing Ltd

First published in Great Britain in 2020
Transferred to digital print in 2024

A catalogue record for this book is available from the British Library.

Print ISBN: 978 1 4728 3826 1
ePub: 978 1 4728 3827 8
ePDF: 978 1 4728 3824 7
XML: 978 1 4728 3825 4

Maps by www.bounford.com
Index by Rob Munro
Typeset by PDQ Digital Media Solutions, Bungay, UK
Printed and bound in India by Replika Press Private Ltd.

24 25 26 27 28   10 9 8 7 6 5 4 3 2

The Woodland Trust
Osprey Publishing supports the Woodland Trust, the UK's leading woodland
conservation charity.

www.ospreypublishing.com
To find out more about our authors and books visit our website. Here you will find
extracts, author interviews, details of forthcoming events and the option to sign-up
for our newsletter.

Dedicated to my grandparents.

CONTENTS

Introduction

On 9 June 53 BC, two worlds collided on a dusty plain outside the town of Carrhae, near the modern-day border of Turkey and Syria. The outcome of the battle that day would reshape the geopolitical map and establish a frontier between East and West that would endure for the next 700 years.

Over the previous three centuries, the republic of Rome – now an empire in all but name – had crushed all opposition in its inexorable rise to power over the entire Mediterranean basin. No people had been able to resist Rome; not its Italian neighbours, nor the Punic civilization of Carthage, the Celtic tribes of Spain and Gaul, the Macedonian heirs to Alexander III of

The front line of battle, as depicted in this relief from the Mausoleum of the Julii in Saint-Rémy-de-Provence, France, was no place for the faint-hearted. The Parthians, peppering the Romans with arrows at the battle of Carrhae, would have beheld a similar vista, with the legionaries bracing for the shock of impact. (Leemage/ Universal Images Group via Getty Images)

This Parthian ceramic relief plaque depicts a mounted horse archer, 1st to 3rd centuries AD. Note that the rider needed both hands to wield the bow; controlling the horse and impelling it to conform to changes in speed and direction could only be achieved through pressure via the knees and heels, such fine-tuning requiring years of training. The Persians – of the Achaemenid, Arsacid and Sasanian dynasties – are, like the Carthaginians, a people without their own history. Even their very name, 'Parthian,' is a western derivation; outside of the archaeological and numismatic evidence, everything we know about them is derived from the texts of their Greek and Roman rivals. This must be borne in mind when discussing the context and course of relations between them. (CM Dixon/Print Collector/Getty Images)

Macedon ('the Great'), the Anatolian states of Pontus, or Armenia. As the Romans thrust ever deeper into the East, however, advancing into the power vacuum left by the implosion of the Seleucid Empire, they would encounter a civilization unlike any they had crossed swords with before.

A new dynasty had arisen in Persia. From their heartland in the steppes of Central Asia, the Parthians had first wrested control of the Iranian plateau from the Seleucid Empire, after which they seized Mesopotamia, establishing their capital at Ctesiphon. The Parthian 'King of Kings' now ruled a federated state stretching from the Euphrates River to the Indus River. Parthia was not looking for a fight, but Rome could tolerate no rival. These new barbarians represented either a threat, if powerful, or an opportunity, if weak; either way, conflict was inevitable.

The Euphrates River which, along with the Tigris River, engendered the birth of civilization itself in Mesopotamia. At the time this photo was taken the Euphrates demarcated the front line between Kurdish Rojava on the east bank and ISIS on the far, western bank. The Euphrates served a similar role for centuries in antiquity, demarcating the boundary between the Roman and Persian spheres of influence. In 1 BC, the consul Gaius Caesar was dispatched to Syria by his grandfather, the Emperor Augustus (r. 27 BC–AD 14). On neutral ground – an island in the Euphrates – and with an equal retinue on each side, he met with the Parthian king Phraates V (r. 2 BC–AD 2). According to Velleius Paterculus, an eyewitness, this spectacle of the Roman forces arrayed on one side, the Parthians on the other, was a truly memorable one (Shipley 1924: 261). (Author's Collection)

1 238 BC: The Parthians under Arsaces I assert their autonomy from the Seleucid Empire.

2 129 BC: The Parthians overwhelm the Seleucids to confirm their suzerainty over Mesopotamia and the Iranian plateau.

3 127 BC: The Parthian king Phraates II is killed in combat against nomads; the long Parthian eastern frontier, exposed to the steppe of Central Asia, will remain vulnerable to incursion.

4 95 BC: First contact between Rome and Parthia.

5 66 BC: Roman triumvir Pompey establishes a treaty of non-aggression with King Phraates III of Parthia.

6 54 BC: Roman triumvir Crassus violates the treaty and invades Parthia, only to be defeated at the battle of Carrhae the following year. A Parthian counter-invasion enters Syria but peters out by 51 BC.

7 40 BC: Seeking to take advantage of the civil war in Rome, Parthian forces under prince Pacorus and the Roman renegade Labienus invade and occupy Syria and Asia Minor. Roman general Ventidius defeats and kills Labienus in 39 BC and Pacorus in 38 BC.

8 36 BC: Roman triumvir Antony invades Parthian client state Media Atropatene. His siege of Phraaspa fails and he is forced into a gruelling retreat through the mountains into Armenia.

9 AD 54: After a long period of peace inaugurated by the Roman emperor Augustus, war breaks out between Rome and Parthia over Armenia. Initial Parthian success is negated when Roman general Corbulo arrives to stabilize the situation. The war ends with the status quo ante restored in AD 63.

10 AD 114: Roman emperor Trajan annexes Armenia. The following year he invades Mesopotamia, takes Ctesiphon and advances to Charax. The Romans are overextended, however, and cannot hold their gains in Mesopotamia. Trajan dies in AD 117 and his successor, Hadrian, pulls the Roman frontier back to the Euphrates.

11 AD 161: Parthian king Vologases IV invades Armenia, defeats local Roman forces and advances into Syria. In AD 164 Roman reinforcements dispatched by Emperor Marcus Aurelius drive the Parthians out; the following year they advance into Mesopotamia and sack Ctesiphon. The Romans advance the frontier to Dura Europos.

12 AD 197: Roman emperor Septimius Severus invades Parthia. Rebuffed at Hatra, he advances into Mesopotamia and sacks Ctesiphon.

13 AD 216: Roman emperor Caracalla advances into Parthia under the pretext of sealing a marriage alliance with the daughter of Parthian king Artabanus V. After massacring the Parthian nobility at the wedding, Caracalla marches unopposed into the Parthian heartland to sack and plunder, desecrating the tombs of the Parthian monarchs at Arbela.

14 AD 217: After Caracalla is assassinated his successor as emperor, Macrinus, must face the wrath of the vengeful Artabanus V. Roman and Parthian forces clash in a three-day battle at Nisibis which ends in stalemate.

15 AD 224: Artabanus V falls in battle with the rebellious house of Sasan. Ardashir I takes the throne in Ctesiphon as first king of the Sasanian line; end of the Parthian dynasty.

It was the triumvir Marcus Licinius Crassus – alongside Pompey and Caesar, one of the three men who shared real power in Rome – who first crossed the frontier and invaded Parthian territory. Unwittingly, he had initiated a conflict that would endure for generations until it became engrained in the national psyches of both combatants, for Rome had finally encountered a people it could not subdue. Rome's legions were masters of the battlefield, from the Rhine to the Nile. As infantry, they had no peers. Crassus, however, was stumbling into a trap, for the Parthians refused to fight by the rules as the Romans understood them. The Parthian mode of warfare – their way of life – focused exclusively on the horse. Marching eastwards, the foot-slogging Roman infantry were about to encounter the hard-riding Parthian cavalry galloping to meet them.

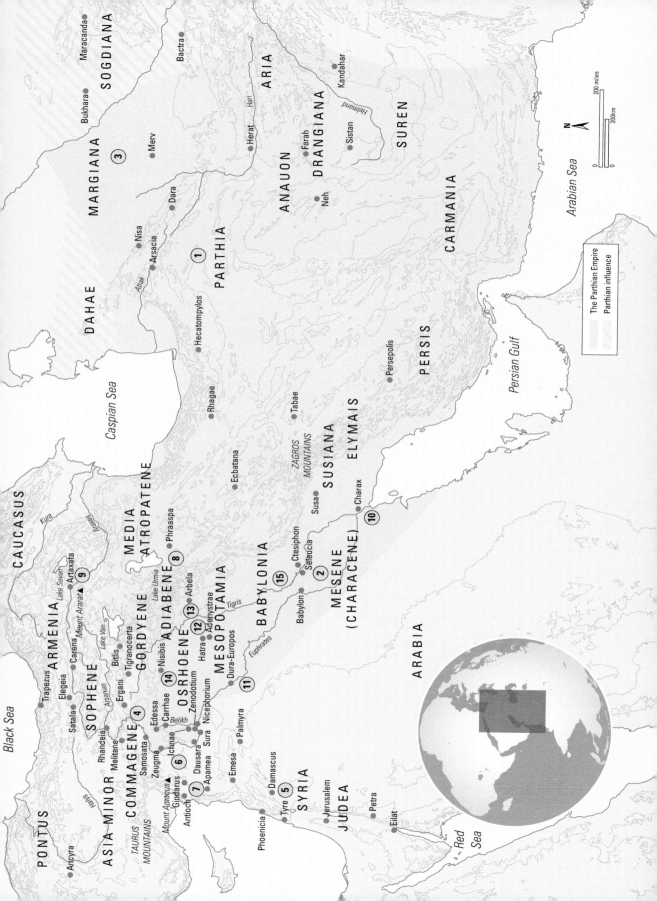

The road to war

The strategic context for the clash between Rome and Parthia lies in their respective geopolitical trajectories; their expansion put them, unwittingly, on a collision course.

The Parthians originated as the Parni, a branch of the Dahae confederation of Scythian tribes, east of the Caspian Sea. Parthian tribute bearers appear on bas-reliefs in the palace at Persepolis built by the Achaemenid king Darius I (r. 522–486 BC) in the 5th century BC; Herodotus lists the Parthians among Xerxes' host confronting the Greeks in the 4th century BC. In the wake of Alexander the Great's conquest of Persia, Diodorus mentions Parthian troops as serving in the army of the Macedonian general Antigonus. At the battle of Paratacene in 317 BC, Alexander's would-be successor stationed 1,000 mounted Parthian archers and heavy cavalry on one flank (Diodorus IX: 307). The land that would form the core of the Parthian state lay within the territory claimed by another of Alexander's generals, Seleucus.

According to Strabo, the inception of the Parthian state dates to when the nomad warlord Arsaces conquered the territory, then a province of the Seleucid Empire; his successors continued to annex the neighbouring kingdoms until Parthia extended from the Indus to the Euphrates (Strabo 11.9.3). With King Seleucus II (r. 246–225 BC) struggling to assert his title, Andragoras, the Persian satrap (governor) in Parthia, took the opportunity to secede around 245 BC and establish his own kingdom. Being aware that Seleucus II was tied down with affairs in Syria and Asia Minor, Arsaces, a warlord of uncertain ethnic origin, invaded Parthia and defeated and killed Andragoras, securing control of Parthia by 238 BC.

Although the two peoples remained entirely ignorant of each other's existence, the Parthians owed their rise to Roman intervention. The Seleucids were able to contain Arsaces' heirs until Roman forces crushed the forces of King Antiochus III (r. 222–187 BC), the sixth ruler of the Seleucid Empire, at Magnesia in 190 BC. In the aftermath, Seleucid authority collapsed, and the Parthians seized this opportunity to expand. After the Parthians wrested Iran and Media from the Seleucids, the critical turning point came in 141 BC when the Parthian king Mithridates I (r. 171–132 BC) invaded Mesopotamia. Defeating the Seleucid king Demetrius II (r. 145–138 and 129–126 BC), Mithridates accepted the surrender of the cities of Seleucia and Babylon. By the time of Mithridates' death in 138 BC, the Seleucid Empire had been driven back west of the Euphrates. The Seleucids staged a brief revival under Antiochus VII (r. 138–129 BC), but in 129 BC their last army was defeated, along with their king. The Parthian king Phraates II (r. 132–127 BC) was now in a position to mop up the rump Seleucid state in Syria, but unfortunately for the Parthians, imminent victory in the west was undermined by a rising threat from the east.

Throughout its history there were two inherent qualities of the Parthian state that repeatedly retarded its capacity for focusing exclusively on the confrontation with Rome. The first was its endemic political instability. The second was the long eastern border that fronted onto the endless expanse of Central Asia. Bereft of geological features that would have demarcated a 'natural' frontier, Parthian territory was perennially exposed to invasion from the steppes. Pressure from the jostling tribes to their north had led to a fierce nomadic people, the Saka, emigrating into the region adjoining the Parthian border. In 128 BC, Phraates II led his army to halt their progress; he was killed, as was his successor, Artabanus I (r. c.127–124/23 BC), who died fighting a second wave of migrating nomads known as the Tochari.

With Parthian prestige in tatters, newly subjected peoples to the east and west rose up. Succeeding to the throne in 124 BC, Mithridates II (r. 124–88 BC) reoccupied Mesopotamia in 122 BC. By 115 BC, when Chinese sources appear to indicate that the Parthians had secured the border city of Merv, he had pacified the eastern frontier, facilitating the establishment of long-distance trade routes with China. The focus of Parthian rule shifted westwards, with the seat of government being transferred to Mesopotamia and a new winter capital city of Ctesiphon, on the Euphrates (the summer capital being Ecbatana in Media).

While the Parthians pushed west, however, the Romans too were on the march. Rome had broken Antiochus III and humiliated Antiochus IV (r. 175–164 BC), but Rome's own expansion into the East was facilitated peacefully when Attalus III (r. 138–133 BC) of Pergamum in western Asia Minor made the republic his legal heir, the Senate annexing the state when he died in 133 BC.

The first diplomatic contact between Rome and Parthia occurred on the banks of the Euphrates in 95 BC, when the Roman statesman and general Lucius Cornelius Sulla met with Orobazus, an emissary of Mithridates II. Sulla, who had just installed Ariobarzanes I (r. 95–c.63/62 BC) as client king of Cappadocia in eastern Asia Minor, insulted the Parthians by arranging that their envoy take a submissive posture seated beneath him and separated from Ariobarzanes, implying that Parthia was both subordinate to Rome and had no credit in Cappadocia. When Mithridates II was advised of this humiliation he ordered Orobazus executed for failing to assert Parthian prestige more vigorously. In any case, no treaty emerged from this initial encounter defining spheres of influence or a commonly recognized frontier between the two states.

Events on both sides rapidly superseded any potential for confrontation between them. In 91 BC the Social War (91–88 BC) broke out between Rome and its Italian allies. No sooner was this resolved than the Romans found themselves at war with Mithridates VI of Pontus (r. *c.*120–63 BC), who bundled them out of Asia Minor. The Romans were unable to respond effectively because in 88 BC civil war erupted between Sulla and his rival Gaius Marius. The Parthians moved into Syria that same year to impose a puppet Seleucid king; but just as they were on the cusp of consolidating their hegemony over the entire Fertile Crescent, the death of Mithridates II in 87 BC plunged the state into ten years of complete anarchy. In the power vacuum created by the retraction of both Roman and Parthian influence, Tigranes II of Armenia (r. 95–55 BC) annexed Syria and the Parthian provinces of Gordyene and Adiabene in Mesopotamia, invaded Media and sacked Ecbatana.

By 74 BC, Rome had recovered its equilibrium sufficiently to settle accounts with Mithridates VI. He forged an alliance with Tigranes II, but two successive Parthian kings – Sinatruces (r. *c.*78/77–70/69 BC) and Phraates III (r. 69–57 BC) – refused to participate in a joint front against the Romans. The allies were defeated by the Roman proconsul Lucius Licinius Lucullus at Tigranocerta in 69 BC and Artaxata in 68 BC.

In 66 BC the Senate dispatched Gnaeus Pompeius Magnus – Pompey the Great – to take charge in the East. In Rome's first formal treaty with Parthia, the two sides pledged non-aggression and non-interference. That same year, Pompey defeated Mithridates VI at the battle of the Lycus, while Phraates III supported the son of Tigranes II (also named Tigranes) in a bid to seize the throne from his father. Parthian forces invaded Armenia, but no sooner had Phraates III crossed the frontier than he withdrew, abandoning the younger Tigranes to his fate. Pompey subsequently marched into Armenia and recognized Tigranes II as the reigning monarch, after forcing him to disgorge the territories he had annexed over the past two decades – Cappadocia, Cilicia, Syria and Phoenicia, as well as the province of Sophene east of the Euphrates – leaving him only the original heartland of Greater Armenia.

Pompey campaigned in the Caucasus Mountains, but his ultimate objective was to create a network of client states among the region's minor kingdoms, from Cappadocia to Osrhoene. His settlement did not extend to the restoration of Gordyene and Adiabene to Parthia from the Armenians. In 65 BC, Pompey's legate Aulus Gabinius raided deep into Armenian territory, crossing the Euphrates and reaching the Tigris. In response, Phraates III invaded and annexed Gordyene. He then sent ambassadors to Pompey demanding a final resolution of the previous year's agreement, including the return of the former Parthian territories from Armenia and confirmation of the Euphrates as a line of demarcation between the two empires.

By way of reply, Pompey demanded that the Parthians evacuate Gordyene. When Phraates III prevaricated, Pompey ordered another of his legates, Lucius Afranius,

The military leader Gnaeus Pompeius Magnus, known to history as Pompey the Great, had already earned his moniker when he set out on what would become his most significant campaign to the East, where he subdued Pontus and restructured the region from Armenia to Judea into a network of client kingdoms subservient to Rome. (Hulton Archive/Getty Images)

to recover the province. The Parthians withdrew their occupying force rather than risk a fight with Rome. Afranius pursued the Parthians back across the Tigris and then returned to Syria by way of Mesopotamia during the winter of 65 BC. In that year, Phraates III again invaded Armenia and waged war on Tigranes II, who was now technically a Roman ally. Although Pompey contemplated an invasion of Parthia, he decided against it. Splitting the difference, Adiabene would be returned to the Parthians while Gordyene – its location offering access to the Parthian heartland – would remain Armenian and, by extension, a strategic Roman asset.

Having reduced Armenia to a client state, annexed Pontus and Syria, subjugated Judea and established a shatterbelt of compliant petty kingdoms the length of the long eastern frontier, Pompey returned to Rome. Only Parthia remained outside the Roman orbit, but so long as Armenia remained subordinate to Rome, and the ancient kingdom of Commagene guarded the crossing points on the upper Euphrates, Parthian expansion westward could be effectively contained. Parthia had weathered the storm, but the portents for the future were ominous.

The Opposing Sides

ORGANIZATION AND COMMAND

Roman

Theoretically, at first contact Rome confronted the feudal patchwork of Parthia with the resources and focused direction of a unitary state. In reality, however, by the 1st century BC the Roman republic no longer possessed a national military under constitutional authority. What it had were a number of private armies, loyal solely to the warlords who raised, funded and led them. The Senate could only retain control over and discipline those second-tier generals who lacked the means to rise higher, men such as the proconsul Lucius Licinius Lucullus and Pompey the Great's legate Aulus Gabinius. Increasingly, the only role left to play for the duly elected but increasingly redundant representatives in Rome was to indulge the ambition of men such as Marius, Sulla, Crassus, Pompey and Caesar with a veneer of constitutional propriety. Only at the conclusion of the civil wars, with the end of the republic and the ascendancy of Octavian Augustus and his principate, could Roman policy be effectively centralized.

Until then, raising an army was the exclusive preserve of Rome's elite as it required political appointment and substantial funds. Crassus, a former consul and head of a business empire with an accumulated fortune in finance, slaves and real estate, was the epitome of this type in the late republic. Once ensconced with proconsular authority in the provinces, far beyond the oversight of the Senate, a governor had virtual carte blanche to undertake military initiatives as he saw fit; blatant imperial aggrandizement could always be retrospectively justified as pre-emptive defence against an imminent threat. Ambition, talent and success fed each other in a mutually reinforcing spiral of martial aggression as victories accrued loot and attracted recruits.

The core of a Roman army was the legion, which as the republic expanded from city-state to empire had been refined through trial and error to its definitive form. The legion's ten cohorts were each sub-divided into three maniples of two centuries. A legion had a total complement of up to 4,800 men on paper, but in practice this was rarely attained, especially by legions that had been on campaign for protracted tours of duty.

The backbone of the Roman Army was Rome's junior officer class, the centurion. There were 59 of these men to a legion, five in the first cohort and six each in cohorts two to ten. In battle each century of approximately 80 men would be led by a centurion on the far right of the front line, a *tesserarius* (sergeant) stationed at the opposite end of the front line and an *optio* (deputy) in the rear rank. A century also had a *signifer* (standard-bearer) and *cornicen* (trumpeter) attached. The *signifer* served as the visual marker for a rallying point while the *cornicen* functioned to relay basic strategic commands, but in the heat of battle each centurion would be expected to respond to threats and opportunities on his own recognizance.

Command of a legion under the authority of the general devolved upon the legate (*legati*); subordinate officers included the *tribuni militum* (military tribunes) and the *praefectus castrorum* (prefect of the camp), the latter responsible for logistics and day-to-day operations. By the last century of the republic the old system by which legions would be raised on an ad hoc basis to meet a particular contingency and subsequently dissolved no longer applied. The legions had become institutionalized, evolving their own collegial identities based on geographic markers, such as Caesar's I *Germanica* and III *Gallica*, or boasts of martial prowess, such as Caesar's VI *Ferrata* ('Ironclad') and XII *Fulminata* ('Armed with Lightning'). The granting of citizenship to Rome's allies in the wake of the Social War (91–88 BC) had also led to the abolition of the *ala sociorum* (the separate legions of the allies). From then on the legions of Rome would be better described as the legions of Italy. Unless

This statue of the Emperor Septimius Severus (r. AD 193–211) is at the UNESCO World Heritage site of Leptis Magna (the ruins of which are in Khoms, Libya), where he was born in AD 145. Tough and unscrupulous, Severus patched together an empire fragmented by civil war, always choosing his moment carefully to eliminate his rivals one by one. The price for stability was to make the Roman Army the true centre of Roman politics. By massively expanding their pay and privileges, Severus was able to keep the legions placated; but the imperial treasury could not sustain this policy, and successive emperors would pay the ultimate price. (De Agostini/Getty Images)

faced with a supreme crisis, however, a Roman general would never stoop to inducting non-Italians into a legion; these served in their own distinct units as *auxilia* (auxiliaries).

The legions were defined by their flexibility in terms of formation as individual units composed of identically trained and equipped men who could adjust to the tactics of the new enemies and the environments of the new battlefields the armies of the republic were encountering as they probed ever further from their Mediterranean heartland. A well-drilled army could deploy in squares as easily as lines. Generals communicated with their officers via couriers or through the display of the *vexillum*, a rectangular coloured banner mounted on a pole; where necessary, communications would be relayed through the *signifer* and *cornicen*. There were two classes of standard: those used as rallying points for individual maniples; and the *aquilae*, the eagle standard that represented the legion as a whole. Bearing this standard was a great honour, and its loss a terrible disgrace.

The frontier system as evolved by the Emperor Augustus was based on armies permanently established on the frontiers and able to move when necessary to any trouble-spot. From the reign of Hadrian (r. AD 117–138), the legions became static, committed to specific provinces. The Emperor Septimius Severus (r. AD 193–211) intensified this attachment to a particular locale when he allowed the legionaries to marry legally. Mobility was intended to be retained through the hiring of local peoples as distinct *numeri* (units) and increasing use of *vexillationes* (detachments) from a number of legions, which would return to their base once a specific task had been completed. By the end of the 2nd century AD, however, this no longer sufficed to meet the demands of maintaining the far-flung frontiers of the empire. Severus had to raise three entirely new legions in order to amass enough manpower for his campaigns against Parthia without compromising the garrisons on the Rhine and Danube. In addition to expanding the total size of the Roman Army, he made recruitment more attractive by endowing the individual legionaries with their first increase in pay since the reign of Domitian (r. AD 81–96). More soldiers, needing more money; this was the first cycle in an accelerating spiral of inflation and instability that would nearly tear the empire apart by the end of the 3rd century AD.

Parthian

Parthian society was feudal in nature. The power of the Arsacid kings was both dependent on and limited by the vast private armies maintained by the other great noble families of the realm: the Suren, Mihran, Kiran, Zik, Kanarangiya, Ispahbudhan, Spandiyadh, Jusnaf and Andigan. Most of these houses were Parthian in origin, but the empire accommodated indigenous Persian and immigrant Greek interests, while the Suren were of the Saka tribe of Sistan. Alongside the Mihran and Karin, the Suren were the most powerful of the houses, asserting the hereditary right to crown the Arsacid king, a privilege they retained even under the successor Sasanian dynasty.

The rudimentary Parthian state apparatus therefore lacked the functionality of its Roman rival in terms of a professional bureaucracy, a tax revenue stream and a standing army. For it to function at all required an assertive king authoritative enough to keep the nobility in line so that when he summoned them and their retainers to join his household troops on campaign, whether offensive or defensive, they came. Even in the best-case scenario, therefore, Parthian warfare operated on an ad hoc basis, their armies living off the land as opposed to maintaining a logistical chain. For this reason, Dio notes, the Parthians were almost invincible in their own territory and in any that had similar characteristics, but while they occasionally scored some successes in pitched battles and in sudden incursions outside of their natural habitat, they could not wage an offensive war on a sustained basis (Dio III: 427–429).

In time of war, the Parthian elite were expected to commit their private armies of personal retainers to serve the collective interest of the state, each of the great houses contributing a number of horsemen proportionate to their wealth and status. The reciprocal relationship between service on the part

This Indo-Scythian coin, dating from the second half of the 1st century BC, captures the essence of the horse-archer combination that ruled Central Asia for thousands of years and was a constant threat to the sedentary cultures to the west, south and east. The Arsacid dynasty of Parthia was one of the most successful, and enduring, of the steppe peoples, carving out a state that dominated Mesopotamia and the Iranian plateau for over four centuries. Note the prominent *gorytos* (combination quiver and bow-case) slung behind the rider, allowing for easy access to arrows. (Ashmolean Museum/Heritage Images/ Getty Images)

This depiction of a Scythian archer on horseback both pre-dates and reflects the Central Asian origins of the Parthian dynasty and its mode of warfare. By the 1st century BC, the Parthians were powerful enough to go toe-to-toe with the Romans of that time, as Dio observed from the perspective of the 3rd century AD; and even in his day, they remained a match for the Romans (Dio III: 425). This grudging regard never translated into admiration, however. Much trade passed across their long common border, but to the end, they remained two separate cultures, two distinct identities, two closed worlds. (CM Dixon/Print Collector/ Getty Images)

Dura-Europos, photographed from the air during inter-war excavations led by Yale University. Occupying a strategic location in territory contested between Rome and Persia, the city changed hands numerous times. Founded in 303 BC by the Seleucids on a 90m-high escarpment above the right bank of the Euphrates River to control the trade-route crossing, Dura-Europos fell to the Parthians in 113 BC. The Emperor Trajan (r. AD 98–117) took the city in AD 114; it reverted to the Parthians in AD 121, then in AD 165 was again taken by the Romans, who used it as an advanced forward base for operations against the Parthian heartland in Mesopotamia. After a bitter siege in AD 256 the Sasanian Shah Shapur I (r. AD 240–270) sacked the city; it was subsequently abandoned. (Yale University)

of the common people and obligation on the part of the nobility was deep-rooted and intimate, with the latter being expected to raise the former 'as carefully as their own children,' Justinus explains, 'and teach them, with great pains, the arts of riding and shooting with the bow' (Justinus XLI: ii).

The largest Parthian army mentioned by the sources is the 50,000-strong royal army mobilized against the Roman general Antony. It can be assumed that Parthian armies followed established steppe nomadic practice, being divided into units of ten, 100, 1,000 and 10,000 men, each led by its own commander according to his place in the feudal society. The small company was called *wašt* (*c*.100 men?), a regiment *drafš* (*c*.1,000 men) and a division *gund* (*c*.10,000 men). The whole army (*spād*) was under the supreme commander – the king, his son or a *spādpat* (general-in-chief) chosen from one of the great houses.

TROOP TYPES, WEAPONS AND EQUIPMENT

Roman

A legionary kept a *pugio* (dagger) at his belt for close-quarters combat, but his primary offensive weapons were his *gladius* (sword), a straight and double-edged cut-and-thrust weapon approximately 60cm long, and his *pilum* (javelin), which reached up to 2m in length. Through generations of trial and error the *pilum* had been refined as a throwing weapon. Its narrow point and long, thin iron shank were designed for penetration, and upon impact the shank would distort, twisting downward under the weight of the shaft, not only making it impossible for an enemy to retrieve and hurl back at its owner but rendering the victim's shield unusable.

In addition to his body armour and helmet, for personal protection each legionary carried a *scutum* (large shield) 66cm wide, at least 1.1m long and as thick as a man's palm. It was composed of planks of wood glued together rather like modern plywood, surrounded by an iron rim that could withstand blows on its edge, and with an iron *umbo* (boss) running down its length, thicker in the middle, that could be used offensively to punch an opponent.

Each legion had attached to it approximately 300 cavalry divided into ten squadrons of 30 horsemen, each squadron being commanded by a *decurio* (troop commander). Most of Rome's cavalry needs were met by *auxilia* from foreign nations, primarily Spaniards, Africans, Celts and Germans. The same applied to light-armed and missile troops, Cretan archers and slingers from the Balearic Islands being popular choices.

The shock of Rome's defeat at Parthian hands spurred innovation. The Romans learned to deploy more missile troops to keep the Parthians at bay, especially slingers, whose stones could bring down even the cataphracts (armoured

The head and shoulders of a centurion survive in this fragment of a marble relief, probably from the Temple of the gens Flavia on the Quirinal Hill, now in the National Museum, Rome. Centurions were expected to lead from the front, and suffered disproportionate casualties as a result. (De Agostini/Getty Images)

This legionary, a veteran of Legio V *Alaudae*, has served under Mark Antony ever since the Ides of March, 44 BC. He has only ever experienced victory on campaign before, but now finds himself caught up in the desperate retreat from the failed siege of Phraaspa through the high mountains of Armenia in 36 BC. In the struggle to keep the ever-elusive Parthian foe at bay, he is poised to throw his primary offensive weapon, the *pilum* (javelin).

Weapons, dress and equipment

About 2m long overall, consisting of an iron shank about 7mm in diameter and 60cm long with a pyramidal head, the *pilum* (**1**) had an effective range of up to 30m when cast. It could also be retained for close-quarters combat, but the preferred weapon of the legionary when closing with the enemy was his sword, the *gladius* (**2**), a straight and double-edged cut-and-thrust weapon approximately 60cm long and slung in a scabbard from his belt at the right hip. In case of emergencies, a legionary also kept a dagger, the *pugio* (**3**), from 18–28cm long and 5cm or more in width, slung in a scabbard from his belt at the left hip.

For personal protection, each legionary carried a large oval shield, the *scutum* (**4**). It was composed of planks glued together rather like modern plywood, surrounded by an iron rim that could withstand blows on its edge, and with an iron boss running down its length, thicker in the middle, that could be used offensively to punch an opponent. The emblem of Legio V was an elephant, but its cognomen, *Alaudae*, was derived from its origins in Caesar's Gallic Wars.

This legionary wears a standard Montefortino-style helmet (**5**). The horsehair plume rising from the helmet signified a particular sub-unit, and could be black, white or red. Standard issue for Roman legionaries of the late republic was chainmail armour (**6**), worn over a simple tunic. These – and the openwork, hobnail boots, or *caligae* (**7**) – provide little protection against the elements as the season wears on towards winter and the climb into the mountains becomes more arduous; many more legionaries will die of illness and exposure than from enemy action during the retreat.

Dating from the 1st century BC, the tombstone of Annaius Daverzus, an auxiliary who served with cohors IIII *Delmatarum* on the Rhine frontier, on display in the Museum Roman Hall, Bad Kreuznach, Germany. Note he is carrying two spears, thus increasing his options for the deployment of missiles vs close-quarters weapons. (Birgit Gierth/ullstein bild via Getty Images)

cavalry) encased in armour that kept them immune to arrows. Armies became more balanced, with the foot-slogging legions of infantry supported by greater numbers of cavalry recruited from peoples such as the Sarmatians, specialist horsemen rivals to the Parthians in the saddle; and the legionaries themselves evolved over time. Helmets transitioned from the Montefortino style to the Coolus type. Body armour slowly converted from the chainmail of the republic to the *lorica segmentata* (segmented cuirass) of the principate. The shift within the legions to the form they would take in the late empire – the legionaries back in chainmail, now wearing trousers and bearing oval shields, wielding longer swords and longer spears more suitable for engaging cavalry at a distance – was just beginning to take effect when Rome fought its last war with Parthia.

This is the only known surviving example of the semi-cylindrical Roman legionary *scutum*. Dating from the 3rd century AD, it was discovered during excavations at Dura-Europos. Other than the missing central *umbo* (boss) it is complete, even including the original painted decorations, which reflect Roman iconography of victory, such as a lion and an eagle with a laurel wreath. (Yale University)

COMBAT Parthian horse archer

Reflecting the more decentralized basis of their culture, there was no uniformity in any Parthian army, each warrior riding to the fray outfitted to the best his status and means allowed. Nevertheless, we can with some confidence reconstruct a typical exemplar of the Parthian host that routed the Roman invasion of 36 BC. This man is steering his horse away from the enemy at full gallop while simultaneously turning around in the saddle and firing back over the hindquarters – the legendary Parthian Shot, from which the term 'parting shot' is derived. The level of coordination required to make this tactic work – and not in isolation, but synchronized with hundreds or even thousands of fellow mounted warriors, under battlefield conditions – speaks to the almost symbiotic relationship between man and beast that defined the Parthian way of war.

Weapons, dress and equipment

The primary weapon of the horse archer was the powerful composite bow (**1**), constructed from layers of wood, horn and sinew. The Parthians loosed their arrows from the right side of the bow, and employed the thumb draw common to peoples of the Eurasian steppe. To facilitate this, horse archers wore thumb rings that allowed the bowstring to ride smoothly over the thumb during the release without chafing the skin. Note that this figure has a trio of arrows clutched in his bow hand ready for fast transfer to the string for his next three shots (**2**). The typical Parthian arrow was fashioned from cane, glazed and painted. The bow was slung at the waist from the belt in a *gorytos* (**3**), a combination quiver and bow-case, together with a reserve supply of arrows (**4**). An axe, short sword or, as in this case, a dagger (**5**) was carried at the belt as a secondary, close-quarters weapon.

Eschewing protection for speed, this unarmoured Parthian horse archer is accoutred in a stylized variation of Scythian-style dress, from his leather or (in this case) felt kaftan shirt (**6**) to his boots (**7**). Leggings like cowboy chaps were worn to protect the inner thighs (**8**); these were very baggy, hanging in tightly draped folds held up by two suspenders attached at the back. Individuals might ride with their heads unencumbered save for a headband, or in this case wear a felt hooded cap (**9**).

The most important adjunct to the horse archer was, of course, his horse. This would be of the Nisean breed, minimally accoutred. Crucially in the absence of stirrups, balance would be maintained through use of the horned saddle (**10**), the four prongs of which enabled the rider to shift his weight appropriately and guide his mount through pressure applied via the knees.

Parthian

The Romans recognized that the Parthians – fundamentally an equestrian culture – were the product of their environment. As Dio noted, the flat terrain they inhabited was ideal for the breeding and use of horses (Dio III: 427). Their characteristic mount was the Nisean horse, a now-extinct breed once native to the town of Nisa, located in the southern foothills of the Zagros Mountains in Iran. From childhood, a Parthian male was defined by, and had his inherent worth evaluated on the basis of, his qualities in the saddle. 'They ride on horseback on all occasions,' Justinus adds; 'on horses they go to war, and to feasts; on horses they discharge public and private duties; on horses they go abroad, meet together, traffic, and converse' (Justinus XLI: iii). On campaign, a Parthian army would incorporate far more horses than men. Each rider would have several horses in reserve, enabling him to always have a fresh mount available when an opportunity arose to seize the critical moment on attack or be able to withdraw at speed when threatened.

Second only to his skill on horseback was a Parthian's talent with the bow. This emphasis on archery was another corollary of the climate in the Parthian heartland, for as Dio explains, the hot, dry summer weather, bereft of moisture, was vital to keeping their bowstrings taut (Dio III: 427). For that reason, whenever possible, the Parthians avoided campaigning in winter.

Eschewing protection for speed, the unarmoured Parthian horse archers were dressed in a variation of Scythian costume consisting of a leather or felt kaftan, trousers and boots. Leggings like cowboy chaps were worn to protect the inner thighs; the chaps were very baggy, hanging in tightly draped folds held up by two suspenders attached at the back. Individual horse archers might sport a Scythian-style *bashlyk* (cap) or prefer to ride unencumbered save for a headband.

The primary weapon was the powerful, recurved, composite bow, constructed from layers of wood, horn and sinew. The wooden core formed the frame, with strips of buffalo horn laid on the inside to resist compression. The sinew – dried, broken into fibres, saturated in glue and layered on the

Horses graze beside the ruins of the ancient University of Harran and the minaret of the Grand Mosque (Ulu Camii) in Harran (ancient Carrhae). The definitive Parthian mount was the Nisean horse, a now-extinct breed once native to the town of Nisa, located in the southern foothills of the Zagros Mountains in Iran, and first bred by the Medes. The Akhal-Teke breed from Turkmenistan is believed to be their descendants. (Martyn Aim/Corbis via Getty Images)

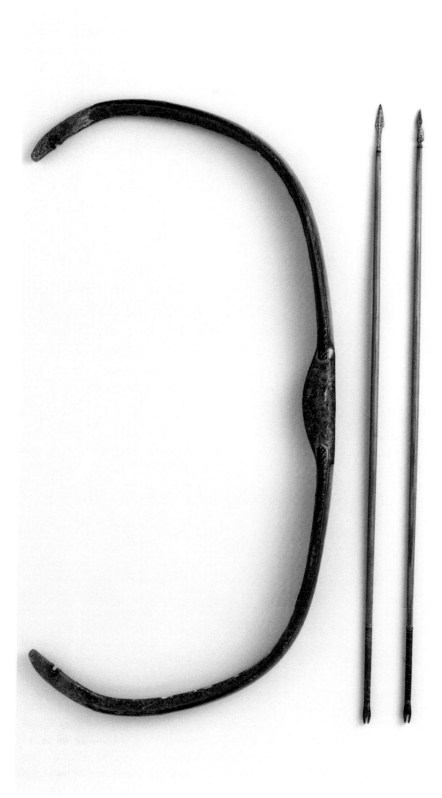

This exemplar of a composite bow from the Metropolitan Museum of Art, New York, illustrates the tremendous latent power of the weapon in its relaxed, unstrung state. When strung, the tips (ears) of the bow would be pulled back against their natural curve (i.e. the arrows would be aimed from right to left in this illustration). This would generate significantly greater velocity than a simple self-bow while still being compact enough to be wielded on horseback. Such bows were constructed through painstakingly gluing together the component pieces of wood, horn, and the sinews of animals in a process that could take months or even years. (The Metropolitan Museum of Art, New York: Rogers Fund, 1935)

A Parthian cataphract takes on a lion in this panel now held by the British Museum, London. The rider is fully encased in armour, but the helmet does not enclose the face. Note the couched lance; this method of delivering the weight of horse and rider into the blow pre-dates the invention of the stirrup. (British Museum/Wikimedia/Public Domain)

outside – resisted tension. The tips (ears) of the bow were extended and stiffened with horn, which increased tension and helped control the release. In this way, tremendous energy was stored during the draw and unleashed when the arrow was loosed.

The Parthians employed the thumb draw common to peoples of the Eurasian steppe. To facilitate this, horse archers wore thumb rings that allowed the bowstring to ride smoothly over the thumb during the release without chafing the skin. The bow was slung at the waist from the belt on the left side in a *gorytos* (combination quiver and bow-case) together with a supply of arrows. Axes, short swords and daggers were carried at the belt as secondary weapons.

The nobility at the core of the Parthian state constituted the cataphracts, the heavy cavalry of the warrior elite. In the account of Justinus, the armour of the cataphracts, 'and that of their horses, is formed of plates, lapping over one another like the feathers of a bird, and covers both man and horse entirely' (Justinus XLI: ii). The effect, according to Heliodorus, was to create the impression of a living, moving statue (Hadas 1957: 231). The psychological impact of encountering this hypnotically terrifying sight, in witnessing thousands of mechanical warriors on the move in full battle array, was profound. Ammianus Marcellinus, a historian of a slightly later generation, described how the coats of armour worn by the close-order groups of Parthian cavalrymen reflected the sunlight, dazzling onlookers (Rolfe 1940: 461). Nazarius relates how the Emperor Antoninus Pius (r. AD 138–161), renowned for his abilities in peacetime and a capable war leader, had mobilized for a campaign against Parthia, but was so intimidated by the sight of the cataphracts massed for battle that he sought peace from their king; this offer was spurned, though Rome ultimately emerged triumphant, but it was evident that the cataphract's armour engendered confidence in the wearer and fear in his opponent (Anderson 2016: 61).

The primary weapon of the cataphract was the *kontos* (lance), which in the absence of stirrups was supported by a loop at the horse's neck, while its butt was fixed by a noose to its hindquarters at the croup. Through this arrangement, the shock of impact was absorbed by the mount, not by the rider. Heliodorus explained that when used in this way, the *kontos* could achieve impressive penetration, even being able to transfix two of the enemy in one thrust (Hadas 1957: 231). The cataphracts also carried two-edged longswords, axes and maces.

DOCTRINE AND TACTICS

Roman

A Roman army would construct a fortified camp for security at the end of each day on campaign. A typical Roman field camp was 800m square and surrounded by a ditch 3.7m wide and 2.7m deep. The earth from the ditch was used to build a parapet which was then studded with sharpened wooden stakes to present a spiked front to any would-be aggressor. Inside the perimeter the tents of the soldiers and their officers were arranged so that each unit always occupied the same location and was grouped in combat formation for rapid deployment.

Every legion contained specialists in engineering and construction so that, if given time, a Roman army could construct bridges, manufacture siege equipment and build transport or even combat vessels. Although bonuses might be forthcoming upon completion of particular tasks, no-one ever got rich on a legionary's salary, which barely covered expenses. The real money

Dating from the 2nd century AD, this sarcophagus relief is a composite reflecting differing modes of cavalry warfare. The figure is wearing the helmet and *lorica musculata* ('muscle cuirass') of a high-ranking officer, but he carries no shield and his horse is not fitted out with a saddle. These latter qualities were characteristic of the light-cavalry auxiliaries Rome recruited from allied or subject peoples, such as the Numidians, who wore no armour but could dart in and out of the front lines, throwing javelins as depicted here. (DEA/A. DAGLI ORTI/ De Agostini via Getty Images)

was in loot and plunder, of both goods and human beings for the slave markets; hence the appeal of a bold, visionary and successful commander. Ambition may have been the driving force for those warlords engaged in pushing the frontiers of Rome ever deeper into the unknown, but greed was the motivation of those men who flocked to their standards.

Typically, each legion would form up for battle in three horizontal lines (the *triplex acies*), the front line consisting of four cohorts, its centuries arranged ten wide by eight deep, the second and third lines of three cohorts each, their centuries arranged 12 wide by six deep. The intervals between the centuries were necessary to maintain cohesion and to prevent them dissolving into a disorganized mass. It was easier for an army to advance and maintain formation if this was carried out by small mobile units acting in unison rather than by a huge and unwieldy continuous line.

The legionaries were encouraged to beat their *scuta* (shields) with their *pila* (javelins) as they advanced and utter a collective war cry as they closed to contact with the enemy. The noise – shouts and screams – as two armies clashed in battle would have been deafening. In the press of combat under these conditions, officers could only resort to yells and hand-signals to convey orders.

However well-drilled, experienced and professional the legions, however strong the *esprit de corps* of the legionaries, battle was therefore always a gamble. Vegetius counselled that a truly qualified commander would consider every alternative, from ambush to attrition, before rolling the dice on a set-piece engagement (Clarke 1767: 116). A succession of wars with Parthia offered an ideal proving ground to distinguish Rome's good commanders (Ventidius, Corbulo) from the bad (Crassus, Paetus).

The Parthians were expected to be manageable opponents when Crassus first crossed the Euphrates in 54 BC because Lucius Licinius Lucullus had easily defeated mounted archers and armoured cataphracts in Armenia at the battle of Tigranocerta in 69 BC. Lucullus had ordered his lightly armed auxiliary cavalry to charge the Armenian cataphracts and keep them occupied

while several hundred legionaries rushed forward to surround their position. The legionaries were instructed to strike at the unprotected legs of the enemy's armoured horses, causing the riders to tumble from their heavy mounts. The much larger Armenian army was routed, further convincing the Romans that their infantry-focused approach to war was inherently the superior model. This attitude accurately reflects Roman arrogance as the legions marched due east from Carrhae – but they were about to discover, at considerable cost, that their one-size-fits-all approach to warfare did not apply in Parthia.

Parthian

As it closed to contact, a Parthian army was typically composed of a five-part array, consisting of an outer left, left, centre, right and outer right, all capable of independent action, with the baggage train and spare horses stationed to the rear. The essence of Parthian warfare was mobility:

> They fight on horseback, either galloping forward or turning their backs. Often, too, they counterfeit flight, that they may throw their pursuers off their guard against being wounded by their arrows. The signal for battle among them is given, not by trumpet, but by drum. Nor are they able to fight long: but they would be irresistible, if their vigour and perseverance were equal to the fury of their onset. In general they retire before the enemy in the very heat of the engagement, and, soon after their retreat, return to the battle afresh; so that, when you feel most certain that you have conquered them, you have still to meet the greatest danger from them. (Justinus XLI: ii)

This relief from the 1st century BC depicts a famous moment from Roman legend. When an earthquake in 362 BC opened a chasm in the Roman Forum in Rome, an augur warned that it could only be closed when the gods received in sacrifice the most precious possession of the city. The citizens despaired until they were rebuked by a young soldier named Marcus Curtius, who pointed out that the answer was embodied in the arms and courage of the Romans themselves. Mounting his horse, fully armed and armoured, he plunged into the chasm, which closed over him, thus saving Rome. This fable emphasized the martial traditions and code of honour that inspired generations of Roman imperialism. (DEA/A. DAGLI ORTI/De Agostini via Getty Images)

Standard tactics offered four basic options. First, the army could adopt a crescent formation in order to outflank and surround the enemy on both wings. Second, the Parthian forces could mass to one side in order to outflank the enemy on one wing. Third, the Parthians could make use of a convex array to break the enemy's centre. Fourth, the Parthian army could carry out a feigned flight to draw the enemy into an ambush.

The Parthians favoured the first option because this enabled them to subject the enemy to a barrage of arrows from all directions. In this manner, Crassus came to grief at Carrhae. When the enemy was surrounded, cavalry archers would trot towards their formation, loosing arrows ahead of them, until breaking into a gallop approximately 100m from contact. As both hands were required to use the bow, each horseman, now at full speed, was controlling his mount using nothing more than his knees and heels while continuing to load and loose arrows. Once within 50m of the front line they would wheel through 90 degrees, presumably to their right, so they could circle the enemy formation, loosing arrows to their left into the packed ranks of the foe. That compensated for the one blind spot of the cavalry archer, who could cover a 270-degree angle from horseback – to his front, left and rear – but could not effectively shoot to his right. We can therefore assume that the Parthians who shot the legions to pieces at Carrhae were circling them in an anti-clockwise direction.

Lucan noted that the exclusively cavalry character of Parthian warfare proffered both a tremendous advantage in tactical mobility on open terrain and a corresponding aversion to campaigning in rough country: 'The Parthian in Sarmatia's plains/Where Tigris spreads across the level dunes/Contends invincible, for flight is his/Unbounded; but should uplands bar his path/He scales them not …' (Lucan VIII: 420–24). This perspective was exaggerated, however; while the Parthians certainly preferred to fight on the flat plains of Mesopotamia, they could hold their own against any Roman commander who underestimated their tactical flexibility in the valleys and mountain passes of Armenia. Classical accounts of Parthian warfare are also as significant for what they leave out as what they account for. The bulk of

A period tapestry depicting horsemen out hunting. The riders are clearly based on Parthian motifs; each wears a Scythian-style *bashlyk* (cap), while the central figure wields a composite bow from the saddle. European cavalry carried a shield into combat to protect the rider, leaving one hand free to grip sword or spear. There was no place for a shield in Parthian warfare, however. A horse archer needed two hands free to load and fire his bow, and relied on the speed of his mount for protection. The cataphract needed two hands free to wield his *kontos* (lance), and counted on the strength of his armour to ward off blows. (The Metropolitan Museum of Art, New York: Gift of George F. Baker, 1890)

Although it is synonymous with their culture, the Parthian (i.e. Parting) Shot, in which the archer turns in the saddle to loose an arrow backwards over the hindquarters of his horse, long pre-dates the Parthians themselves, as the figures from this c.500 BC Etruscan bronze cinerary urn demonstrate. The harmonization of man and mount was the signature manifestation of Parthian warfare, reflecting the convergence of its culture with its geography. Dio described how the Parthian warriors practised archery from an early age, in an environment that favoured equestrianism and the use of the bow (Dio III: 427). The open steppe was the ideal environment in which to refine tactics emphasizing mobility and killing from a distance. On more than one occasion this left the Romans struggling to come to grips with the Parthians. (The Metropolitan Museum of Art, New York: Joseph Pulitzer Bequest, 1940)

Parthian infantry consisted of subject peoples, mercenaries and other non-Parthians – Armenians, Greeks, Indians and Roman deserters. Because of the Parthians' exclusive emphasis on the use of cavalry in set-piece battle, the Romans would typically only encounter Parthian infantry during siege actions against enemy camps, forts and cities. The Romans themselves were secure behind the battlements of their cities, which rendered the Parthians impotent. Justinus noted their lack of siege craft (Justinus XLI: ii), a lacuna in their strategic capacity to project power also highlighted by Lucan: 'They fill no hostile trench, nor in their hands/Shall battering engine or machine of war/Dash down the rampart; and whate'er avails/To stop their arrows, battles like a wall …' (Lucan VIII: 429–32).

The fundamental weakness of the Parthian war machine was therefore its limited range of available strategic alternatives. Owing to the nature of Parthian society, everything was invested in the mobility and firepower of the horse archers coupled with the overwhelming force of the cataphracts. If battle was offered on terms favourable to this combination, it was lethal; but if not, there was no alternative to fall back on.

Carrhae

53 BC

BACKGROUND TO BATTLE

In 58 BC, Pompey's former legate Aulus Gabinius was elected consul and governor of Syria. Either that year or the following, Phraates III was murdered by his two sons Mithridates and Orodes. Mithridates, being the elder, took the throne under the title of Mithridates IV. The parricides then fell out; Mithridates IV was ousted in a coup by a faction of the nobility led by the Surena, who then installed Orodes II as king (r. 57–37 BC). Orodes then married Laodice, daughter of King Antiochus I of Commagene (r. 70–38 BC). The tightening of ties between these two states was significant, for as Josephus notes, Samosata, the capital of Commagene, served as an ideal jumping-off point for any excursion across the Euphrates (Whiston 1895: 697).

Mithridates IV, meanwhile, fled to Syria, pleading to Gabinius for intervention on his behalf. After getting as far as the Euphrates, however, this expedition came to an abrupt end when the governor, in return for a large bribe, opted to restore another forlorn royal exile, Ptolemy XII Auletes, who had first reigned in 80–58 BC, to the throne of his kingdom, Egypt, for a second reign in 55–51 BC. Mithridates IV returned home alone to raise the standard of rebellion against his brother, while Gabinius was recalled to Rome and prosecuted for exceeding his authority.

Gabinius was succeeded by Marcus Licinius Crassus, who made no secret of his intention to carry forward the aborted invasion of Parthia. Annexing Mesopotamia would mean the accession of rich territories to the republic, and guarantee access to the Persian Gulf and a direct trade route to the Indies. The emasculated remnant of Parthia would remain a tributary ally of Rome, with a client king on the throne.

Given the unbroken string of Roman victories in the East under Lucullus and Pompey, Plutarch (288) notes that those who had enlisted under Crassus were quite sanguine that the Parthians would offer no greater challenge than the Armenians; the Romans anticipated that the most difficult part of the war would lie in the tedium and frustration of pursuing an opponent who refused to fight at close quarters. There were many in Rome who opposed a conflict with Parthia, however, being uneasy with the fact that one man's private obsession would embroil the state in a war against a people who had offered no provocation. Crassus left Rome to take up his command in late 55 BC. As he approached the city gates, one of the tribunes, Gaius Ateius Capito, ordered him arrested. When this failed, Ateius pronounced anathema on the entire expedition, prophesying its inevitable doom. Ateius was subsequently prosecuted for reporting these omens, but acquitted on the count that the result of the subsequent battle had shown them to be true.

By mid-54 BC, Crassus and his army had arrived in Syria and were preparing to invade Parthia. Some of Crassus' men had served with Pompey in the 60s BC, but most would have been relatively raw, certainly in terms of service in the East. After crossing the Euphrates, Crassus sought out the Parthian satrap of the region, Sillaces, and engaged him in battle near the town of Ichnae. The Parthians were routed, Sillaces himself being wounded. Crassus secured his grip over northern Mesopotamia by garrisoning the key strategic towns of the region with 7,000 infantry and 1,000 cavalry. Ichnae, Nicephorium and Carrhae went over to the Romans voluntarily; Crassus sacked Zenodotium and sold the inhabitants into slavery. He then withdrew into Syria, spending the winter of 54/53 BC

The distinctive 'beehive'-style houses of present-day Harran (ancient Carrhae). Though the walls that once surrounded this location are now long gone, the contours of the flat, open surrounding country – ideal for cavalry warfare – have remained unchanged over the past 2,000 years. Plutarch (392) exaggerated when he asserted the Romans were marching into a sea of sand in 53 BC. The clouds of dust kicked up by tens of thousands of tramping feet and galloping hooves would, however, play a major part in the ensuing battle. (De Agostini/Getty Images)

squeezing funds from the major cities and looting the Great Temple of Jerusalem in Judea.

The ancient sources criticize Crassus for being too cautious and not pressing on into southern Mesopotamia to support Mithridates IV and take control of the cities of Seleucia, Babylon and Ctesiphon. It was at this moment that Crassus committed his first, and greatest, error, Plutarch notes (390), for he lost this opportunity effectively to dismember the dysfunctional Parthian state. Crassus may have been awaiting reinforcements, particularly his son, Publius, who was serving with Caesar and was on his way at the head of 1,000 Gallic cavalry; but in his absence, the Surena advanced into southern Mesopotamia, took Seleucia and Babylon and captured Mithridates IV, dispatching him to his brother Orodes II, who promptly ordered him executed.

When Crassus drew his army out of winter quarters in the spring of 53 BC, an embassy arrived from Orodes II. The ensuing exchange was less than diplomatic. The King of Parthia professed to take pity on an old man's folly, and, in deference to Crassus' advanced age, would allow his army to depart in peace (Plutarch 390–91). Crassus scornfully retorted that he would make his reply to Orodes II after the Romans arrived in Seleucia, upon which Vagises, the senior ambassador, laughed and, striking the palm of his left hand with the fingers of his right, retorted that hair would grow in that spot before Crassus laid eyes on Seleucia.

Disturbing reports were indeed coming in from the Roman garrisons stationed in Mesopotamia about the nature of the Parthian host assembling there. Moving so swiftly that it was impossible for Roman forces to evade them or to catch them if they chose to flee, the Parthian horse archers could pierce the Romans' armour with their arrows without revealing their positions; and

Founded as a Macedonian colony in 304 BC, Carrhae, in the region of Osrhoene, was a sizeable market town situated at the crossing of two main caravan routes linking Syria with the Tigris Valley from west to east and the Halys Valley with southern Mesopotamia from north to south. (Martyn Aim/Corbis via Getty Images)

the Parthian heavy cavalrymen wielded formidable edged weapons and wore impregnable armour (Plutarch 391).

Artavasdes II, King of Armenia, arrived in the Roman camp with the 6,000 horse of his life-guard and a pledge to provide 10,000 more cavalry and 30,000 infantry. He urged Crassus to invade Parthia via Armenia. This would not only allow for more secure lines of supply; advancing through the mountains would negate the Parthian advantage in cavalry. Some of the officers did counsel caution, in particular the quaestor, Gaius Cassius Longinus. Crassus, however, was determined to take the direct route, and crossed the Euphrates at Zeugma with seven legions of infantry, 4,000 cavalry and an equal number of lightly armed auxiliary troops.

Aware that Orodes II was in the field, Crassus again elected against taking Seleucia, Babylon and Ctesiphon. Marching south would have been to risk being trapped between those cities and the royal Parthian army roaming unhindered behind him. Crassus needed a decisive battle, and marched east looking for one. Keeping to the line of fortified towns with Roman garrisons, Crassus followed a major caravan route towards the Belikh River, a tributary of the Euphrates. Word then arrived that Orodes II, determined to knock Artavasdes II out of the war before he confronted Crassus, had invaded Armenia; the Romans could not expect any reinforcements from that quarter. On the other hand, in pursuit of his strategic objective, Orodes II was apparently willing to sacrifice Mesopotamia to buy him the time he needed. The only Parthian forces remaining in the region were the 10,000-strong personal retainers of the Surena, whom Orodes II had presumably ordered to shadow and harass the invading army; given he was outnumbered 4:1, it is very unlikely that Orodes II expected the Surena to confront Crassus, let alone actually defeat the Roman.

This marble sarcophagus of the 1st century BC depicts a Roman prefect, Tiberius Flavius Miccalus, with two soldiers of his escort. The prefect is receiving his helmet; note the long *spatha*-style cavalry sword hanging from his right hip. In ancient times, the extent to which the mounts of the cavalry were endowed with defensive protection varied from culture to culture. In the East, with its emphasis on heavy cavalry as the elite core of the army, this could be extensive, with armour completely covering the horse as well as the rider. In the West, particularly in Rome, where the infantry was the decisive arm, cavalry could go into combat completely unprotected, though those who could afford it might fit their horse with a chamfron to protect its head. Accordingly, Roman cavalry could not stand up to the charge of the Parthian cataphracts, as Crassus discovered to his great cost at Carrhae. (DEA PICTURE LIBRARY/De Agostini via Getty Images)

1 Having crossed the Belikh River on June 9, Crassus, aware the Parthians are approaching, draws up the army in a hollow square, fronted on all sides by 12 cohorts of legionaries, each supported by skirmishers and a troop of horse. Crassus commands from the centre of the formation, with Cassius deputed to one wing, Publius the other.

2 The Parthians come into sight. The Surena orders his cataphracts to charge in order to pin the Romans in place.

3 The Parthian horse archers encircle and surround the Roman square.

4 Crassus orders his light infantry to disperse the Parthian horse archers; they are repulsed by a hail of arrows.

5 With his static position under incessant missile fire, Crassus orders his son, Publius, to take 1,300 horse, 500 lightly armed auxiliaries and eight cohorts of legionaries to charge the Parthians.

6 The sortie under Publius is drawn away from the main Roman body, isolated, and wiped out.

7 As night falls, the Romans set up a field camp. Under cover of darkness, they slip away, abandoning those too wounded to march.

8 At around midnight, 300 Roman cavalry under Egnatius arrive at Carrhae, give notice that the rest of the army is in retreat, and ride off for Zeugma. The garrison commander, Coponius, dispatches patrols to escort Crassus into the town.

9 At dawn on June 10, the Parthians descend on those Romans left behind at the field camp and slaughter all of them.

10 While rounding up stragglers from the Roman night march, the Parthians corral and eliminate four cohorts under Varguntinus. A handful of survivors are allowed to escape so the Parthians can track their flight.

11 The Parthians arrive at Carrhae.

12 As night falls, the Romans again attempt to break out. Led astray by their guides, the Romans make fitful progress.

13 Cassius with 500 cavalry makes it back to Syria.

14 Octavius leads 5,000 men into the relative safety of the high country of Sinnaca.

15 At dawn on June 11, Crassus is still on the road with four cohorts of legionaries and a few cavalry. He is intercepted by the Parthians and only saved by the intervention of Octavius.

16 During a parlay between Crassus and the Surena, negotiations break down; Crassus is killed. The remaining Romans flee; most are run to ground.

Battlefield environment

Known today as Harran, Carrhae already had an ancient lineage in 53 BC. The town was a major node on an important thoroughfare spanning the Fertile Crescent, linking Damascus to Nineveh and Carchemish. It is mentioned in Assyrian inscriptions as early as the time of Tiglath-Pileser I (r. 1114–1076 BC), and was the stronghold of the last Assyrian king until the final fall of his empire to the Medes in 609 BC. The Achaemenid Persians assumed authority over Carrhae until its conquest by Alexander in 331 BC. It was then inherited by their Seleucid successors until the collapse of that dynasty, when it passed under the suzerainty of Osrhoene, ruled by the Arabian Abgarides as a client state of Parthia. Crassus, therefore, was far from entering into an unknown void when he crossed the Belikh River; he was marching along one of the oldest established trade routes on Earth. Nor was the environment particularly hostile. It was summer, and hot; there was no shade, and tens of thousands of tramping feet and hooves would kick up great clouds of dust, but the terrain was grassland interspersed with scrub. The army could march by day, beasts could graze and men would not be falling out of the line with sunstroke or dehydration. The fact that Crassus would be so completely surprised and outmanoeuvred by the Surena was not due to his crossing some geographic boundary into an alien world, but was entirely a consequence of his failure effectively to balance his army with the combined arms necessary to counteract the mobile nature of Parthian warfare.

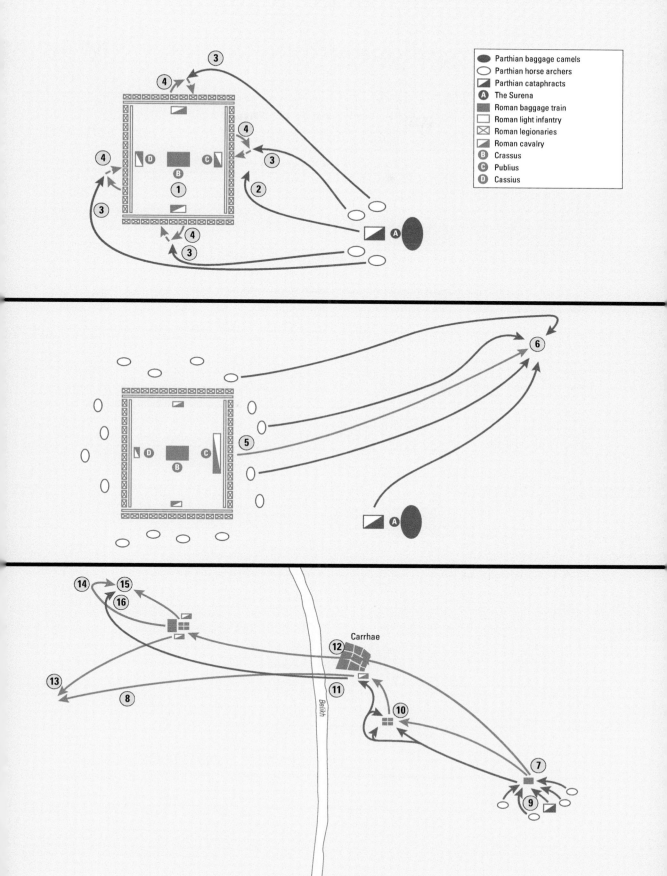

⬤	Parthian baggage camels
⬭	Parthian horse archers
◪	Parthian cataphracts
Ⓐ	The Surena
▮	Roman baggage train
▯	Roman light infantry
⊠	Roman legionaries
◪	Roman cavalry
Ⓑ	Crassus
Ⓒ	Publius
Ⓓ	Cassius

Carrhae

Belikh

A coin of Orodes II (r. 57–37 BC). Note the seated figure on the reverse, an image brought to life by his son, murderer and successor, Phraates IV (r. 37–2 BC). When that monarch received ambassadors from the Roman triumvir Antony in 36 BC, Dio describes them being ushered into his presence while the Persian monarch lounged on a golden throne, plucking his bowstring (Dio V: 397). (Classic Numismatic Group, https://www.cngcoins.com/)

INTO COMBAT

On 9 June, Crassus' scouts at last encountered their Parthian equivalents, and were worsted in the ensuing skirmish. Crassus now had to a make a key tactical decision; whether to keep moving, or camp by the river and wait until the following day before pressing on. Crassus wanted to fight. He gave orders to mount up and march out.

With contact imminent, Crassus tinkered with his tactical formation. At first, as Cassius advised, he opened up the files of the legions to stretch his line as long as possible, with the cavalry distributed on each flank, to avoid being surrounded. Then, changing his mind, he drew up the army in a hollow square, fronted on all sides by 12 cohorts of legionaries, each supported by skirmishers and a troop of horse. Crassus commanded from the centre of the formation, with Cassius deputed to one wing, Publius the other.

Their first impression of the Parthians as they rode into view along the horizon did not leave the Romans unduly anxious, for the Surena had clad his cataphracts in coats and animal skins, both to prevent the sun reflecting off their armour and avoid giving away their position as they approached, and also to create a false impression of poverty and barbarism. The Surena then utilized three tactical initiatives in psychological warfare. First, Plutarch describes how, when the Surena gave the signal, the air was filled with the thunderous, unearthly noise of kettle-drums, a sound quite unlike that made by the Romans' brass instruments. Second, he commanded his cataphracts to cast off their ragged garments, revealing a glittering array of polished steel and brass armour. Third, he ordered a charge at the Roman line, which veered away at the last moment; in a classic manifestation of steppe warfare, the Parthians retreated and appeared to disperse, but instead moved to surround the Roman formation before Crassus' men could respond (Plutarch 393). From its opening moments, the Surena had succeeded in ensuring the forthcoming battle would be fought entirely on his terms.

Crassus was now surrounded. He ordered his skirmishers to charge, but they had not gone far before being repulsed by the overwhelming firepower of the Parthian horse archers. The auxiliaries retreated behind the legionary shield wall, but to their dismay, this afforded no shelter. The Roman model of war had always marginalized archery because it had coevolved with the simple self bows of Europe. The velocity generated by the Parthian compound bow was orders of magnitude more powerful. Shocked, the Romans could only watch in horror as arrows started punching right through their shields, their armour and then their flesh.

The Parthians were free to shoot from all sides of the Roman square. Their bows were deadly at a range up to about 150m, and the Romans were packed into such close order that the horse archers could loose their arrows into the massed ranks of the enemy at will, without having to aim at any particular target. The Roman situation was already desperate; in standing their ground they were being shot to pieces, but if they broke ranks and charged out against their tormenters the Parthians simply wheeled and galloped away, firing back over the hindquarters of their horses in the legendary Parthian Shot (which lives to this day in the phrase 'parting shot').

The Romans were not defeated yet; grimly, they held on to one fervent hope – that this onslaught they were being subjected to could not last forever. Surely the foe did not have an unlimited source of ammunition? When their quivers were emptied, they would have to withdraw. This was the conclusion the poet Lucan drew in his *Pharsalia*: that the Parthians lacked both the capacity to prolong their missile assaults and the courage to stand and fight once their supply of arrows was exhausted:

> Wide sweep their horsemen, fleeting in attack
> And light in onset …
> Nor do they dare a combat hand to hand;
> But as the winds may suffer, from afar
> They draw their bows at venture. Brave men love
> The sword which, wielded by a stalwart arm,
> Drives home the blow and makes the battle sure.
> Not such their weapons; and the first assault
> Shall force the flying Mede with coward hand
> And empty quiver from the field. (Lucan VIII: 433–443)

Prince Pacorus of Parthia, son of Orodes II, led three invasions of Roman territory, in 51 BC, 40 BC and 38 BC. These incursions were all ultimately repulsed, Pacorus finally losing his life in battle with the Roman general Ventidius at Gindarus in Cyrrhestica, northern Syria. By force of character, he seems to have represented a real threat to Roman hegemony over the region. According to Dio, Ventidius subsequently pacified Syria, which had been hesitating while awaiting the outcome of the war, by displaying the prince's head in the major cities; the Syrians were unusually fond of Pacorus as he had won a reputation for just governance (Dio V: 383). (Classic Numismatic Group, https://www.cngcoins.com/)

The Surena had planned ahead for just this contingency, however. His baggage train of camels was loaded with spare shafts. When the front ranks of the horse archers had discharged the arrows they carried, they peeled off to restock their quivers (and, though unstated, surely also obtain water for both man and mount) and then returned to the fray.

Thanks to the camels, which the Surena presumably had distributed at well-spaced intervals for ease of access, the aerial onslaught could indeed continue indefinitely. A Parthian cavalry archer could loose an estimated 8–12 arrows every 60 seconds. The Surena brought approximately 9,000 cavalry archers to Carrhae; assuming 1,000 of this number were being rotated out of the line every minute to restock their quivers from the baggage train, then the Roman square was being subjected to a hail of 64,000–96,000 arrows every 60 seconds, or 3.8 million to 5.8 million arrows an hour. In reality, however, no pre-industrial society could have manufactured or distributed such a prodigious quantity of missiles, let alone expended it on this scale. While the initial volleys of the Parthian assault may have approached the averages cited, this weight of incoming shot could not have been sustained. As the battle evolved, the Parthians would have become more selective in choosing their opportunities; when fighting flared up in one sector, there would inevitably have been lulls elsewhere.

For the beleaguered legions, gasping and parched under the blazing sun, there was no respite and no escape. The thousands of galloping horses would have torn up the earth surrounding them, raising clouds of dust that obscured the enemy from sight; the shouts of officers desperate to rally and re-form the lines would have been lost in the thunder of hooves; the pounding vibration in the earth would have resonated in every Roman breast, swelling panic and despair.

Seeing no alternative, Crassus ordered his son Publius to lead a sortie in a bid to drive off at least some of the enemy. Taking with him 1,300 horse (including the entire Gallic cavalry contingent he led to his father from Caesar), 500 lightly armed auxiliaries and eight cohorts of legionaries, Publius

Carrhae, 53 BC

Parthian view: From a Parthian point of view, the enemy at Carrhae amounted to a stationary mass of shields. Roman sorties were swiftly driven back to the main body, their efforts as impotent as the *pila* ineffectually hurled at the elusive horse archers by the tightly packed legionaries. It was characteristic of the Romans, who prided themselves on the structured and methodical nature of their way of war, to denigrate their Parthian rivals as lacking in discipline and self-control. A Parthian army was far from being a mere mob of men on horseback, however; the high-speed, high-risk nature of Parthian warfare demanded a lifetime spent in training the body and mind, to achieve an instinctive partnership between each rider and his horse, and between each mounted warrior within a tactical formation. Members of the detachment of horse archers depicted are careful to remain a single bow-shot from the Roman front line and to maintain contact with each other while keeping well spaced to avoid collision as they gallop parallel to the Roman shield wall. Note that their assault in this sector is coordinated. To avoid friendly fire, the horse archers to the right of the advance detachment will loose plunging shots, up into the sky and then down into the rear ranks of the enemy; at this moment, however, members of the advance detachment aim direct shots right into the front ranks.

Roman view: All most of the Romans at Carrhae can see are the clouds of dust being kicked up by the hooves of the Parthian horses. At seemingly random intervals, Parthian horse archers will gallop out from this screen to pepper the Roman ranks with a barrage of well-chosen shots, and then disappear back into the haze. The strength of the legion depends upon its cohesion, but in these unprecedented circumstances, even the famed Roman discipline is on the verge of complete collapse. The increasingly dehydrated and exhausted legionaries in the front ranks have no good options. They have thrown their *pila* (to little effect), they have no archers or slingers to engage the enemy at a distance, and the Parthians will not approach to close quarters, making their swords useless. If they stand their ground, they will be shot to pieces, as Parthian arrows continue to punch right through their shields. Goaded beyond endurance, some legionaries have broken ranks to chase after a detachment of horse archers who have ridden in temptingly close. The Parthians will allow them to draw just near enough to ensure each of their arrows finds a target. Behind the front ranks, two tribunes have met in a desperate impromptu council of war about what they can do to retrieve the situation. Neither has any answers.

charged the surrounding Parthians. These gave way, and the exultant Romans pursued them until they were out of sight of the main body of the army they had left behind. The Romans were, of course, being led into an ambush. The horse archers herded them into a killing zone. Parthian arrows rained down into the Roman ranks, nailing hands to shields and feet to the ground. At the head of his mounted troops Publius charged once more, but the Roman cavalry were completely outmatched by the cataphracts. The Gallic horsemen fought valiantly against great odds; with their own spears and javelins useless against cataphract armour, they would seize the Parthians' lances in a bid to wrench the riders from their mounts. Or, abandoning their own horses entirely, they would creep under those of the enemy to stab them in the belly, bringing down both beast and rider.

There was to be no escape, however, and the survivors of this foray were forced to retire among the foot, bearing with them Publius, who was grievously wounded. They gathered to make a last stand on a low rise. The end was not long in coming. Publius, his injuries denying him even the dignity of taking his own life, begged one of his attendants to end his misery; many others committed suicide. The Parthians finished off any who continued to offer resistance, taking the rest – not more than 500 in total – as prisoners. Having cut off the head of Publius, they rode off directly towards Crassus.

Publius had at least bought his father some time. The pressure on the main army had lifted as many of the Parthians had been drawn away to consummate the ambush. Publius had dispatched messengers once he realized his predicament; the first were intercepted by the enemy and slain, but one detachment finally got through and reported that Publius and his men were doomed unless they received immediate support. Crassus was paralysed, trapped between a father's desperate desire to rescue his son and a general's duty to ensure the well-being of the army as a whole.

Just as Crassus had finally issued the order to advance, the Parthians returned with the head of Publius, spitted on a spear for all to see. They mockingly inquired as to where his parents were, and who his real family was, professing disbelief that so brave and gallant a warrior could be the son of so pathetic a coward as Crassus.

A bronze *lorica musculata* and helmet, now in the collection of the Metropolitan Museum of Art, New York. This set dates from the 4th century BC, but Roman generals continued to wear such personalized body armour as a stylistic affectation and symbol of their rank throughout the history of the republic, so Crassus may have worn a similar set at Carrhae. Note that the *lorica musculata* has a slight flare at its lower edge; this would have allowed for greater comfort for the wearer while sitting in the saddle. The horse-head decorations on the hinged cheek-pieces of the helmet further imply that the original owner served in the cavalry. (Prisma/UIG/Getty Images)

This bust of Marcus Licinius Crassus is held in the Louvre, Paris, France. Although the ancient chroniclers attributed Crassus' downfall at Carrhae to his avarice and his ambition, this verdict ignores several relevant facts. First, Crassus was, within the bounds of his elite social class, a self-made man. When the Roman general Gaius Marius seized Rome in 87 BC and instituted a purge of potential rivals, Publius Licinius Crassus and his eldest son, Publius, were among the victims. Marcus, the younger son, fled to Spain and raised an army of 2,500 men, pledging himself to Marius' rival, Lucius Cornelius Sulla. Second, there is no doubt Crassus could fight. At the battle of the Colline Gate on 1 November 82 BC, Sulla placed Crassus in command of his right wing. In 71 BC, Crassus led Rome's legions in a campaign that completely destroyed the slave revolt of Spartacus. Third, Crassus was by no means the junior partner to Julius Caesar and Pompey in the triumvirate they forged. All three men were endowed with the right to make war and peace as they saw fit. (cjh1452000/ Wikimedia/Public Domain)

Crassus refused to break. Passing through the ranks of his men, he exhorted them to fight on. His personal courage was not reciprocated, however, for according to Plutarch (395), only a handful of Romans responded; when Crassus exhorted them to raise their voices in a defiant cheer, their faltering response was lost amid the triumphant war cries of their enemy.

Only nightfall saved the Romans. A field camp was constructed in the twilight, but once darkness fell, discipline began to break down. The disintegration started at the top. Leaving the dead where they lay, heedless of the groans and cries of the wounded, or the importuning of his subordinates, Crassus wrapped himself in his *paludamentum*, the red cloak of the *imperator*, and shut down completely. His key officers, Cassius and Octavius, on their own recognizance convened with the centurions and tribunes. Agreeing that the best – indeed only – option was retreat, they ordered everyone still under arms mustered and marched out, abandoning those too wounded to walk.

Progress was agonizingly slow. At about midnight, 300 horse under Marius Egnatius arrived at Carrhae; pausing only long enough to give a brief, garbled account of the previous day's disaster, these rode off at full speed to Zeugma. This was enough to alert the garrison commander, Coponius, who ordered his men to the walls and sent out patrols to escort the battered remnants of the field army into the town.

The Surena was aware that the Romans had displaced during the night, but elected not to risk intercepting them in the dark. Dio notes that this was because the Parthians never encamped near even the weakest of foes as they did not fortify their positions overnight and their mobile archery tactics were impeded by night-time conditions (Dio III: 441). At first light, however, they rode into the Roman field camp and massacred all 4,000 of the wounded who had been left behind. They then spent the rest of the morning rounding up the many stragglers who had strayed from the column during the retreat, including a sizeable detachment of four cohorts under Varguntinus, which was pinned down to a small hill and eliminated with the exception of 20 men who fought their way out. According to Plutarch (395), the Parthians, admiring the courage of these men, opened their ranks to the right and left, and let them pass without molestation to Carrhae. This was probably a tactical gambit, the Parthians hoping to trail the survivors in order to track down the whereabouts of Crassus and the main Roman force.

The following day, the Surena arrived at Carrhae. Crassus could have held the town – he had his own army plus the unbloodied garrison behind its walls, while the Surena, travelling light, had no siege equipment – but Carrhae was not provisioned, and its occupants were too demoralized to make a stand. Crassus' officers urged him to abandon his empty hopes of aid from the Armenians and continue the retreat. That night the Romans set out again, but Crassus was deceived by his guides, who led him into treacherous ground. Losing all faith in Crassus, his subordinates began to carve up the army in order to save whoever they could. Cassius with 500 horse made it back to Syria. Octavius led 5,000 men into the relative safety of the high country of Sinnaca. Daybreak found Crassus still on the road with just four cohorts of legionaries and a very few horsemen. He was less than 2.5km from Octavius when the Parthians descended on him; only the intervention of Octavius saved him from being overrun.

Marcus Licinius Crassus

By the time Crassus assumed command in Syria in 54 BC he had not taken the field since the defeat of Spartacus some 17 years earlier. Then there was the question of his age. According to Plutarch (390), Crassus was 60 years old when he arrived in Syria, and he looked even older than he was. He himself tried his best to make light of it, for example in an incident during the last ritual ceremonies to bless the campaign. When the priest handed him the entrails of the sacrificed beast, they slipped through his fingers and fell to the floor. Aware that this was an ill omen, Crassus laughed and made light of the situation, assuring the horrified witnesses that his sword-hand was sure (Plutarch 391).

Up to a point, Crassus did seem to have a firm grasp on his responsibilities as general; there is no question of his behaving unprofessionally or of allowing any slackness or ill-discipline to compromise the battle-readiness of his army during its occupation of Syria in the year prior to Carrhae. Crassus was swiftly proved to be out of his element once he crossed the Euphrates, however. He did well to establish garrisons in northern Mesopotamia in 54 BC, but surrendered the strategic initiative by not occupying the great cities of southern Mesopotamia while civil war raged there, and he made no attempt to cultivate allies. Mithridates IV would have made a viable client king; but Crassus abandoned him, guaranteeing that he would face a unified Parthian state the following year.

By refusing the Armenian offer of partnership in 53 BC, Crassus both left that country to its own devices (unsurprisingly, it came to terms with Orodes II, leaving Crassus isolated) and chose an invasion route across flat, open terrain that exposed his army to the Surena. If he undertook any intelligence assessments of his enemy he must have ignored them; even the reports coming in from his garrisons warning of the power of Parthian archery made no impression. The composition of his force was wildly unbalanced, incorporating far too few cavalry, and none of the slingers necessary to keep the Parthians at a distance. His tactical dispositions were dubious, his mood swung between over-aggression and irresolution, and finally he collapsed completely, losing control of his fragmenting army.

The ultimate character flaw of Crassus was not his ambition, but his pride. Having risen to the pinnacle of business, military and political power in the Roman world, Crassus could – or would – not come to terms with the alien reality that confronted him at the battle of Carrhae on 9 June 53 BC. His ignominious death in the aftermath of the battle was the inevitable corollary.

The Surena elected to be diplomatic. With his chief officers he rode to the Roman line, unstrung his bow and held out his hand, offering Crassus a truce and safe passage out of Mesopotamia. Crassus was suspicious; he told his men that if they held out until nightfall, they could escape into the high country without having to rely on Parthian good intentions. The remnant of his force had lost patience, however; they mutinied, clashing their shields with their swords in a threatening manner until their erstwhile commander agreed to parlay with the Surena.

What happened next has provoked debate for more than 2,000 years. According to Plutarch, the Surena arrived on horseback with his entourage, and in greeting Crassus remarked on the fact that the Roman general was dismounted. Crassus replied, mildly enough, that there was no error committed on either side, for they both met according to the custom of their own country. The Surena then got down to business. He informed Crassus that Orodes II was prepared to offer peace and a new treaty, but that Crassus must accompany him to the Euphrates to sign it, as the Romans had proved that they could not be trusted to uphold the terms of any agreement (Plutarch 397). Crassus ordered one of his horses be brought, but the Surena told him there was no need, for the Parthian king had provided a suitable mount, and immediately a horse with a golden bit was presented to him (Plutarch 397). Crassus was forcibly put into the saddle by the Parthian grooms, who ran by the side and struck the horse to gee it up. Octavius came running up to

This striking statue of a Parthian aristocrat, on display in the National Museum of Iran in Tehran, is often associated with the Surena. In the sources, the victorious general at Carrhae is identified only by the title of his clan, the Suren – located in Sistan (present-day Sakastan in south-eastern Iran) – so he is referred to as 'the Surena'. As well as being one of the families on the Council of Elders, which confirmed the choice of monarch, the House of Suren also had the hereditary privilege of placing the crown on the head of the new king, which could easily translate into a veto over his taking power. In 53 BC the Surena was not yet 30 years of age, but already renowned for his wisdom. He was second only to the king in terms of his pedigree, wealth and prestige, and unsurpassed in the beauty of his physical appearance; his carefully arranged hair, use of cosmetics and ornate clothing belied his formidable military ability (Plutarch 392). The Surena did not lack for physical courage; when he took Seleucia in 54 BC, thereby ending the rebellion of Mithridates IV against his brother Orodes II, he was the first to scale the city walls. (Raimund Franken/ullstein bild via Getty Images)

seize the bridle, followed by the other Roman officers. This scuffle quickly degenerated further into a brawl; Octavius, drawing his sword, killed one of the Parthian grooms before being hacked down from behind by another. Reinforcements began to arrive on both sides. Dio suggests that the Parthians emerged the victors from this skirmish because they had been primed beforehand to offer assistance to their party before the Romans on the high ground could intervene. Crassus thus met his end, killed either by one of his own men to prevent his being captured, or by the Parthians because he was too badly wounded to survive being abducted (Dio III: 447). The remaining Romans fled; most were run to ground in the aftermath.

This account raises more questions than it answers. Was the Surena empowered to speak for his king? There is no way that Orodes II could have received word of the Parthian victory, let alone determined the terms of the surrender. Was the Surena sincere in seeking to end the conflict, or was he setting Crassus up? Did the Roman officers intervene in a kidnapping attempt, or did they blunder into a cultural misunderstanding and spike the last chance for peace?

Crassus' head was cut off; some accounts maintain that the Parthians poured molten gold into his mouth in mockery. The Surena dispatched Sillaces with the head of Crassus to Orodes II, while parading his Roman captives through the streets of Seleucia in a mocking parody of a triumph. A prisoner resembling Crassus was seated on a horse dressed in women's garments, heralded by lictors who bore the severed heads of the Roman dead suspended from their axes. Behind them trailed local women singing scurrilous and abusive songs about the effeminacy and cowardliness of Crassus.

When the news of Carrhae reached Orodes II, he was feasting with Artavasdes II in Armenia. We do not know whether Artavasdes II even gave battle or simply rolled over when the Parthian army appeared. Parthia and Armenia renewed their old alliance, sealed with the marriage between Artavasdes II's sister and Orodes II's son Pacorus. According to Plutarch, the festivities included a performance of Euripides' *Bacchae*. Seizing the moment, Sillaces threw the head of Crassus into the midst of the production, prompting one of the actors to brandish the gory offering while reciting lines from the play (302–303).

The victory belonged entirely to the Surena. Through his brilliant integration of the three 'T's of warfare – the tactic of horse archery, the technology of the composite bow and the open terrain of northern Mesopotamia – he had comprehensively out-thought, and completely out-fought, an invading army four times the size of the force at his disposal. In so doing, however, he had sealed his own fate. The sheer magnitude of his triumph had endowed him with more prestige than an autocracy tempered only by intrigue and murder could tolerate. Orodes II, envious of his subordinate's success, ordered the Surena executed (Plutarch 398). This was of scant consolation to the Romans, however, who had lost 20,000 men killed and 10,000 taken prisoner in the debacle at Carrhae. Retrieving the *aquilae* taken by the Parthians during the battle would obsess Rome for decades.

The battle of Carrhae ranks as one of the most significant in world history, and one of the most decisive in the history of Rome. Like the disaster of

The Surena

As head of his clan, in the feudal environment of the Parthian social milieu the Surena was expected to lead its fighting men on campaign. The wealth of the Suren can be appreciated from the fact that the Surena was able to commit 1,000 cataphracts and a host of horse archers to confront Crassus at Carrhae – at least 10,000 horsemen in total, drawn from his personal retinue – plus the 1,000 camels of his baggage train (Plutarch 392). The Romans, therefore, did not encounter the royal Parthian army; beyond the satrap Sillaces, and whoever else had survived the defeat at Ichnae in 54 BC, those present were exclusively Suren.

Bringing his own private army to the field, composed of his peers among the nobility and his personal retainers from among the common people, all men who had been raised alongside him and served under him his entire life, offered the Surena a critical edge at Carrhae. He and his soldiers had doubtless ridden together countless kilometres, training, hunting and fighting shoulder to shoulder until the rhythms of manoeuvre and combat were as instinctive as breathing. He had intimate insight into, familiarity with and experience of the men he would lead into battle; they had his confidence, and he had their loyalty. All of this contributed to the masterly command and control he exhibited throughout the battle at Carrhae.

This tells only half the story, however. The Surena had a finely honed weapon at his disposal; and given that he was outnumbered 4:1, wielding it effectively was critical. Here, his personal qualities proved themselves.

By marching with an almost exclusively infantry force across open country at the height of summer, Crassus offered him a priceless opportunity. The Surena understood how best to work these factors to his advantage. He appreciated the significance of logistics, and had prepared his baggage train accordingly. He knew the limitations, as well as the superior qualities, of his army, so for example he elected not to continue the battle at night when he might be at a disadvantage. Above all, he proved to be a genius in the application of psychological warfare. His reading of his opponent was perfect; the Romans, from *imperator* to rank and file, had been broken mentally long before they collapsed physically.

The Parthian victory at Carrhae owed nothing to its king – and that very fact condemned the Surena. Whether his death was the standard fate for any over-mighty subject, or whether Orodes II was specifically alarmed or offended by his presuming to offer terms on behalf of his monarch, can never be answered. The murder of the Surena in 53 BC left the house of Arsaces secure on the throne, but the Parthian state might well have had cause bitterly to regret his absence. Roman authority in the East was tottering after the defeat at Carrhae; had the genius of the Surena been empowered to follow up this defensive success with an equally brilliant offensive into Syria, the border between the two rival superpowers might have been drawn not at the Euphrates but at the Taurus Mountains, or even the Bosporus.

the Teutoburger Wald in AD 9, where three Roman legions and their *auxilia* were destroyed by Germanic tribes, it marked the limit of Roman expansion. The inexorable Roman march to the East, which had already chewed up Macedon, Pontus and the Seleucid Empire, came to an abrupt, wrenching and permanent halt.

In the immediate wake of their victory the Parthians did not advance beyond the Euphrates, but did seize the entire country east of it. Then they began to probe into Syria, taking advantage of the fact that its governor was dead and what survived of its garrisons were in no shape, physically or mentally, to do anything other than hunker down behind the high walls of the major cities. Encouraged, Orodes II committed to a campaign of occupation, nominally led by his young son Pacorus, but actually under the command of his general Osaces.

Roman authority in the East was balanced on a knife-edge, for the provinces were disaffected and ready to defect to the Parthians, who shared their way of life (Dio III: 449). It was Cassius who, upon his own recognizance, assumed the authority to meet this threat. Having re-formed the survivors of Carrhae, including at least 800 cavalry, into two legions,

The victory of the Surena at Carrhae was owed as much to his appreciation of logistics as his mastery of tactics. Aware that his horse archers would soon deplete their quivers if they maintained the rate of fire necessary to keep the Romans pinned down, he had stationed baggage camels with fresh stocks of arrows to the rear of his line. These may have looked like this train, on the pilgrimage to Mecca in the early 20th century. (Library of Congress)

OPPOSITE

This relief from the city of Hatra (1st or 2nd centuries AD) depicts a figure wearing Parthian dress and wielding a dagger standing next to a semeion, a standard with religious significance. Hatra would prove a major thorn in successive Roman attempts to pacify Mesopotamia, resisting sieges by the emperors Trajan (AD 117) and Septimius Severus (AD 197). (Roger Viollet Collection/ Getty Images)

he crushed an anti-Roman insurrection in Judea, then moved north to confront the Parthians in the autumn of 51 BC. The Roman statesman Marcus Tullius Cicero, who had just arrived to take up his assignment as governor of Cilicia, wrote with joy to the politician Marcus Caelius Rufus on 26 November 51 BC that Cassius had successfully defended Antioch (Shuckburgh 1905: II.81).

Rebuffed, the Parthians then completely lost the initiative in the heavily forested country surrounding Antigonea. Cassius set a trap on the route of their withdrawal. He stationed cavalry in the front of his line, but posted infantry in hiding on rough ground to the rear. When his cavalry fell back over familiar roads, he drew the army of the Parthians into the ambush prepared for them and cut them to pieces. Among the dead was Osaces. This success was negated when the freshly appointed governor of Syria, Marcus Calpurnius Bibulus, arrived and was promptly defeated in his first battle, Cicero reporting that Bibulus suffered the loss of his first cohort in its entirety, along with the first-line centurion, a bitter blow (Shuckburgh 1905: II.87).

At the end of 51 BC, Pacorus led his forces to Cyrrhestica in northern Syria (between Antioch to the west and the Euphrates to the east) for the winter. Cicero warned that unless there was some kind of diplomatic breakthrough, war of the most serious kind threatened (Shuckburgh 1905: II.125). Bibulus proved he could make up in intrigue what he lacked as a field commander by winning the trust of the Parthian satrap Ornodapates, who had a grudge against Orodes II, urging him to join Pacorus and support his bid for the throne. Deliberately or otherwise, Orodes II got wind of the affair and recalled Pacorus to Parthia.

Carrhae to Phraaspa

The Roman confrontation with the Parthians petered out as Caesar crossed the Rubicon in 49 BC, convulsing the republic with civil war. Upon achieving supreme power Caesar commenced preparations for a major campaign against Parthia to avenge the humiliation of Carrhae, but three days before setting out from Rome he was assassinated on the *ides* of March 44 BC. Orodes II quietly offered support to the conspirators Brutus and Cassius against Antony and Octavian, but it was Caesar's rival inheritors who emerged victorious at the battle of Philippi in 42 BC. Octavian remained in Rome afterwards, while Antony reorganized the client states of the East (and fell under the spell of Cleopatra). A rogue actor took swift advantage of the ensuing power vacuum.

Before the battle of Philippi, Quintus Labienus had been dispatched as ambassador to Orodes II by Brutus and Cassius. Having heard of the defeat at Philippi, Labienus was unwilling to risk throwing himself on the mercy of Antony and Octavian, and so he not only remained in Parthia but also persuaded Orodes II to take advantage of the destabilization of the Roman state, the disaffection of its provinces, the uncertain loyalties of its legions and the distraction of its rulers (Antony choosing to indulge himself with Cleopatra while Octavian struggled for control of the Mediterranean against Sextus Pompey).

Accordingly, Orodes II authorized a Parthian invasion under the joint command of Labienus and Prince Pacorus of Parthia. In 40 BC, this force invaded Syria, held by the two Saxa brothers for Antony. Labienus was repulsed from the walls of Apamea, but won over the garrisons in the surrounding country to his side without resistance, because these consisted of troops that had served with Brutus and Cassius before Antony incorporated them into his legions. These men were only too happy to switch allegiance again. Employing superior numbers, Labienus defeated one Saxa brother in battle (Dio V: 273), while the other fled, fearing the defection of the men under his command because Labienus kept firing pamphlets into his camp urging them to switch sides. Apamea capitulated, followed by Antioch, and then the rest of Syria and Phoenicia bar the coastal city of Tyre, which held out because the Parthians had no fleet. Pacorus then occupied Judea and 'plundered all Jerusalem, and the palace', Josephus relates; 'Nor indeed did what was in the city suffice the Parthians, but they went out into the country, and plundered it' (Whiston 1895: 358). Pacorus deposed Hyrcanus in favour of his brother Aristobulus; he also won over Antiochus of Commagene and Malchus of Nabataea. Labienus meanwhile occupied all Cilicia bar Stratonicea, which held out after a long siege. Mylasa and Alabanda both surrendered in 40 BC on terms but then revolted and massacred their Parthian garrisons; the citizens of Alabanda were chastised, while Mylasa was burned to the ground after it had been depopulated. Roman authority throughout Asia Minor melted away; the governor, Lucius Munatius Plancus, fled his capital at Ephesus and took refuge on one of the Aegean islands.

Now stretching from the Bosporus to the border of India, the Persian Empire at this moment incorporated more territory than at any time since before the age of Alexander the Great. It was not to last. In 39 BC, Antony, still in Greece, assigned Publius Ventidius Bassus to command the Roman riposte. Ventidius had risen from humble origins as a mule-driver for a Roman Army bakery and later as a contractor of mules and carriages to Julius Caesar in Gaul. After the *ides* he raised three legions for Antony.

Labienus, caught off-guard and without his Parthians (who had returned home for the winter), abandoned Asia Minor and retreated back into Syria with his renegade legions. Ventidius, in a forced march with his light troops, pursued and overtook them on the foothills of the Taurus Mountains. Both sides remained encamped there for several days, Labienus awaiting the Parthians and Ventidius his heavy troops. These reinforcements arrived during the same days on both sides. Though Ventidius had prudently camped on the high ground, the newly arrived Parthians rode straight out at dawn, without even waiting to join forces with Labienus, and charged straight up the incline. Ventidius waited until they were halfway up the slope before ordering a charge; with gravity on their side, the Romans crashed into the oncoming Parthians and hurled them downhill. Many of the Parthians were killed in hand-to-hand combat, while others, wheeling about in flight, hurtled into those still coming up the slope, carrying them away in a general rout. The survivors fled into Cilicia, abandoning the renegade army of Labienus, which disintegrated, Labienus himself subsequently being run to ground.

Ventidius recovered Cilicia and ordered his legate Pompaedius Silo to advance with the cavalry and occupy the Amanus pass into Syria. Pharnastanes, a lieutenant of Pacorus in command of a Parthian garrison at the pass, defeated Silo and was on the verge of overwhelming the Romans when Ventidius arrived with the main body of the army. Ventidius posted 18 cohorts outside his camp in a hidden valley, with cavalry stationed behind the infantry. Then he sent a very small detachment against the enemy. By feigning flight, these men drew the enemy into an ambush, the Parthians (Pharnastanes among them) being slaughtered.

The Parthians subsequently withdrew from Syria and Judea, but they were not prepared to abandon their gains so easily. During the winter of 39/38 BC, Ventidius received word that Pacorus had mobilized an army and intended to invade Syria. With his legions still dispersed in their winter-quarters, he needed to buy time to assemble his army, and was awaiting reinforcement by the legions which were stationed beyond the Taurus Mountains in Cappadocia. Knowing Prince Pharnaeus of Cyrrhestica was secretly in contact with the Parthians, Ventidius pantomimed taking his counsel as an adviser on strategy and tactics. He affected being concerned that the Parthians might not ford the Euphrates at Zeugma but instead choose an alternative crossing point further south downriver, because the terrain in this region was flat and ideal country for cavalry, whereas the rough ground around Zeugma was better suited to Roman infantry.

Pharnaeus, and through him the Parthians, were completely taken in by this ruse. In the summer of 38 BC, Pacorus led his army via a circuitous route to the Euphrates, where he spent more than 40 days in preparing materials and constructing a bridge across the river at a point where the banks were quite widely separated. Ventidius utilized this interval to reunite his forces; with this accomplished, three days before the Parthians arrived, he marched to confront Pacorus at Gindarus in Syria Cyrrhestica.

Because Ventidius had not contested the river crossing or attacked the Parthians immediately after they had got across, Pacorus deduced that he was avoiding a fight because he lacked confidence in the men under his command. Ventidius encouraged him in this belief by remaining in his camp after advancing to contact with the Parthians, refusing to offer battle or even respond to the taunts being hurled at him by the increasingly emboldened enemy. Ventidius knew Pacorus was trying to provoke him into sallying outside of the walls in a bid to drive off his tormenters, at which point his units, unstructured and in open country, would be surrounded and massacred. So, finally, Ventidius apparently did just that. He committed a segment of his force to a sortie, and the Parthian horse archers scattered, drawing the Romans after them.

Convinced the camp was now undefended and his for the taking, Pacorus chose to settle the issue by unleashing his cataphracts against it, even though it was on high ground. Ventidius had reserved the bulk of his troops, however, and, again, the Romans caught the Parthians mid-charge as they galloped uphill; according to Florus, Ventidius delayed his assault until the last moment, allowing the Parthians to approach within 400m, apparently channelling them into a constricted space in which the impetus of their charge was blunted (Florus II: xviii). Again, the Parthian cavalry were driven back down the slope. The trump card for Ventidius was his slingers, Dio records, as these troops could operate at ranges that made it hard for their opponents to counter them (Dio V: 383). Pacorus was cut down; although a few men zealously fought to retrieve his body, when these too were slain, all the rest gave way. According to Justinus, 'never did the Parthians, in any war, ever suffer a greater slaughter' (Justinus XLII: iv). According to Festus, Ventidius had avenged the death of Crassus by killing Pacorus on the 15th anniversary, to the day, of the Roman defeat at Carrhae. He then consummated the pacification of Syria by sending the prince's decapitated head on a city-by-city tour (*Breviarum* 17).

Antony arrived at this point to take command, lest he be completely overshadowed by his subordinate. Ventidius returned to Rome where he celebrated his triumph over the Parthians – the first Roman commander ever to do so – on 27 November 38 BC.

The extraordinary career of Quintus Labienus is encapsulated in this coin. A son of Titus Labienus (one of Caesar's favoured legates who defected to Pompey when Caesar crossed the Rubicon in 49 BC), he served Brutus and Cassius after the *ides* of March 44 BC until their defeat at the battle of Philippi in 42 BC, finding sanctuary subsequently with Orodes II, King of Parthia. The reverse of this coin depicts a Parthian cavalry mount (note the prominent *gorytos*), while the obverse boasts the title 'Parthicus Imperator' – an outrage that contravened Roman norms, Dio writes, as Quintus Labienus took this title from the forces he led against his countrymen, as though *he* were confronting the Parthians rather than his fellow Romans (Dio V: 275). (Classic Numismatic Group, https://www.cngcoins.com/)

Phraaspa

36 BC

BACKGROUND TO BATTLE

After the death of Pacorus, Orodes II lost the will to speak and eat. The king eventually settled on his eldest remaining son to succeed him as Phraates IV (r. 37–2 BC), but the heir apparent proved as impatient as he was ungrateful. After his first attempt to murder Orodes II with poison failed, Phraates IV took the more direct route of having his father strangled to death. To ensure his claim to the throne was secure, he then eliminated all 30 of his brothers and any of the nobility he suspected of conspiring against him.

The survivors of this purge fled into exile. One of this number, Monaeses, the powerful Warden of the Western Marches, who owned great estates in Mesopotamia and had been designated *spādpat* (general-in-chief) of the Parthian armed forces, arrived in Antony's camp seeking asylum. Antony, eager to pick up the mantle of Caesar's aborted campaign, mobilized for an invasion, promising Monaeses the throne of Parthia as Rome's client king. In the spring of 36 BC, however, Monaeses returned home, taking with him invaluable personal insight into the physical strength and strategic objectives of the imminent Roman onslaught.

Antony ordered Publius Canidius Crassus with six legions to compel Artavasdes II of Armenia to abandon the alliance he had maintained with Parthia since Carrhae. Canidius then campaigned successfully in the Caucasus. This foundation having been established, in March 36 BC, having left Syria in the charge of Gaius Sosius, and Asia Minor under Gaius Furnius, and having stationed seven legions in Macedonia and one at Jerusalem, Antony set out from Antioch with ten legions and 10,000 cavalry. Cleopatra accompanied him as far as Zeugma and then returned to Egypt. Antony moved on again in mid-April, arriving at Melitene (modern-day Malatya) in early May before heading north and east along the headwaters of the Euphrates to rendezvous with the other detachments of his army in Carana (modern-day Erzurum) in June. In addition to the six legions of Canidius, these included detachments led by Antony's client rulers, most prominently kings Polemon I of Pontus (r. 37–8 BC) and Artavasdes II of Armenia (r. 55–34 BC), the latter of whom brought 6,000 cavalry and 7,000 infantry under his direct command, the rest of his forces being already stationed on the frontier. The key to the ensuing campaign was an enormous siege train, including a 24m ram, for Antony was aware that he would be operating in country devoid of good timber. Antony's host numbered 100,000 men, its backbone composed of 60,000 legionaries alongside 10,000 Iberian and Celtic cavalry and 30,000 troops provided by his clients. Given the scale of this endeavour, the absence of the 20,000 additional legionaries promised by Octavian must have seemed trivial at the time. Nevertheless, the dispatch of excuses in lieu of men from the West left Antony unable to garrison Armenia and thereby guarantee its loyalty.

Antony's strategic objective was to reduce the Parthian vassal kingdom of Media Atropatene. Tactical considerations dictated this choice. The direct route into Parthia led across the flat plain of Mesopotamia, ideal country for Parthian light and heavy horse. The indirect route, keeping to the rugged terrain of the highlands, was better suited to the hard-marching Roman infantry.

If the Parthians made a stand to assert their claim to Media, the Roman army would be able to fight on favourable terms; but if the Parthians abandoned their vassal kingdom to its fate, Media would be incorporated into the Roman orbit to serve as the springboard for a further incursion into the Parthian heartland. In either instance, Antony's first objective would be to take Phraaspa, the capital of Media, wintering there and then renewing the campaign by marching on the Parthian summer capital Ecbatana (Hamadan) the following spring.

Antony's plan was to march east from Carana to the headwaters of the Araxes and Euphrates, then south-east along the far shore of Lake Urmia to Phraaspa. Antony was no doubt following the template laid down by Caesar for the abortive campaign of 44 BC, but in its execution the gulf between the two men would be cruelly exposed. First, Caesar would never have left his rear unsecured, while Antony had done nothing to ensure the loyalty of Armenia in his absence. Second, Caesar would never have divided his forces in hostile terrain whereas Antony, his siege train making his progress painfully slow, split his army to pass on either side of Mount Ararat. He left two legions under Oppius Statianus with the allied detachments under Artavasdes II of Armenia and Polemo I of Pontus to accompany the siege train via the easier but longer route along the valley of the Araxes while he pushed ahead with the main force.

This detail of the statue of a Parthian aristocrat in the National Museum of Iran, Tehran, illustrates the manner in which leggings were worn to protect the inner thighs from chafing during extended periods on horseback. Resembling modern cowboy chaps, these were very baggy, hanging in tightly draped folds held up by two suspenders attached at the back. Note the dagger tucked into the upper fringe of the leggings. (© akg-images/Dr. Uwe Ellerbrock)

1 Having broken winter camp at Antioch in March, Antony marches with ten legions and 10,000 cavalry to Zeugma. Leaving Cleopatra behind, he sets out again in mid-April.

2 Antony reaches Melitene by early May.

3 Antony conducts a rendezvous with the six legions under Canidius and the forces committed by his eastern clients at Carana in June.

4 Antony splits his forces, detaching two legions under Statianus with allied support from Artavasdes II and Polemo I to escort the siege train via the easier but longer route along the valley of the Araxes north of Mount Ararat while he pushes ahead with the main force via the southern route.

5 Antony crosses the frontier into Media Atropatene in late July.

6 Antony commences the siege of Phraaspa in late August.

7 Monaeses, commanding 40,000 horse archers and supported by the king of Media with another 10,000, falls upon the siege train at Gazaca; Artavasdes II abandons the Roman cause; Statianus falls with his two legions; Polemo I is captured by the Medes.

8 Left no alternative but to withdraw prior to the onset of winter, Antony abandons the siege of Phraaspa in mid-October and commences a 27-day fighting retreat to Armenia via an alternative northern route.

Battlefield environment

In calculating his strategic approach for the invasion of Parthia, Mark Antony was determined to avoid making the same mistakes as the ill-fated Crassus. Instead of striking directly across the level plains of Mesopotamia into the Parthian heartland, he would adopt an incremental approach, advancing via Armenia through the rugged terrain of the Lesser Caucasus Mountains to take Phraaspa, capital of Media Atropatene, in order to detach that Parthian client state from its allegiance to Ctesiphon. Once Media Atropatene had been absorbed into Rome's orbit, it could be used as a staging ground for future incursions into Parthian territory, south into Mesopotamia or even east onto the Iranian plateau. In the event, Antony proved no more successful than Crassus. Unwisely, he split his forces, taking his more mobile units and

advancing ahead of his siege train, which was ambushed and wiped out. Antony now found himself deep in enemy territory, forsaken by his erstwhile Armenian allies, and unable to take Phraaspa or tempt it away from its loyalty to the Arsacid throne. Worst of all, the Parthians proved much more adept at fighting in mountainous terrain than he had given them credit for. Unable to forage and with winter approaching, Antony had no option but to withdraw back into Armenia, through country that rose to a height of more than 4,000m above sea level, his men starving, crippled by frostbite and harassed all the way by Parthian horsemen, who picked off stragglers at will. Antony got what was left of his army out of this nightmarish retreat, but his veteran legionaries could not be replaced, and his reputation never fully recovered.

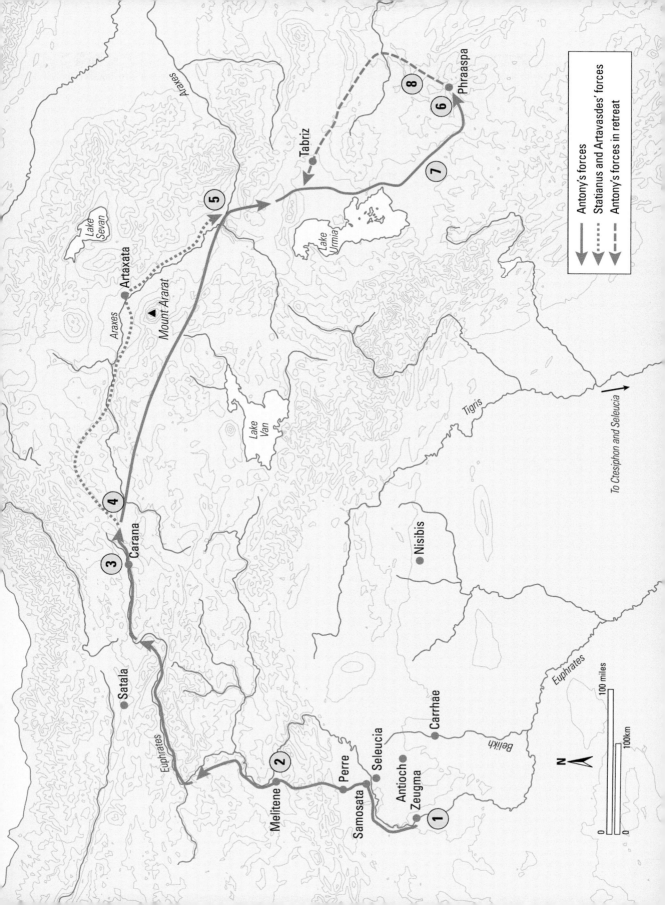

Lake Sevan

Araxes

Artaxata

Mount Ararat

Lake Van

Lake Urmia

Tabriz

Phraaspa

Satala

Carana

Euphrates

Araxes

Tigris

Nisibis

To Cresiphon and Seleucia

Melitene

Perre

Samosata

Seleucia

Carrhae

Antioch

Zeugma

Belikh

Euphrates

N

① ② ③ ④ ⑤ ⑥ ⑦ ⑧

Antony's forces

Statianus and Artavasdes' forces

Antony's forces in retreat

0 100km

0 100 miles

INTO COMBAT

BELOW LEFT
The Palmyrene Gate, the main entrance to Dura-Europos. Although they are synonymous with cavalry and mobility, the Parthians proved adept at constructing fortified positions at least as secure as their Roman equivalents. A Parthian fortress city was built according to a tripartite model. In the centre, in an elevated position, was the *Kohnadezh*, the quarters of the leadership, nobility, and the king that also served as a keep/acropolis. The second section, the *Sharestan*, was the quarters of the knights, petty nobility and men of learning. The third section, the *Savad*, housed the common people. The ideal shape for the fortress city was a circle. (Yale University)

Antony arrived at Phraaspa towards the end of August 36 BC. Monaeses, however, at the head of 40,000 horse archers, supported by Artavasdes I of Media Atropatene with another 10,000, fell upon the second column at Gazaca. Artavasdes II of Armenia, whose cavalry constituted the greater part of the escort for the column, abandoned the Roman cause and rode for home (whether this had been prearranged through covert negotiations with Ctesiphon, or was a spur-of-the-moment decision, remains unknown). The two legions, 10,000 men, fell with Statianus; Polemo I of Pontus was captured; and the siege train, upon which such care had been lavished, went up in flames. Antony, at the first message sent to him by Statianus, rode to the rescue, but as Dio relates, he was too late, finding nothing but corpses when he arrived on the scene (Dio V: 395). He later encountered the Parthian ambush party and drove it off, largely thanks to his slingers, who were deployed in large numbers and whose stones could travel further than the arrows loosed by Parthian archers. Though they could keep the Parthians at bay, the Romans did not succeed in killing many of them, because the Parthians, using their edge in mobility to best advantage, could always avoid any Roman attempt to force them into close combat.

Antony refused to be daunted by this setback. Having established a line of circumvallation around Phraaspa, he ordered construction of a mound against the city walls, and was able to scrape together enough timber to jerry-rig substitute siege engines. However, although doubtless establishing a line of contravallation to keep the main Parthian army at bay, the presence of such a large, mobile force established on his perimeter

BELOW LEFT
This Parthian belt-buckle does a fine job of encapsulating the appearance of its bearer; note the characteristic long hair, tied tight around the brow by a headband but allowed to fall free down the back, and the dagger or short sword carried at the waist. (© akg-images/WHA/ World History Archive)

BELOW RIGHT
Another Parthian belt-buckle. This figure appears to be carrying his bow in his right hand while holding the horse's reins in his left. (© akg-images/WHA/ World History Archive)

severely restricted Antony's options. Far from taking the fight to the enemy, Dio noted, Antony himself was effectively the besieged, not the besieger (Dio V: 397).

Antony did everything in his power to bring Monaeses to bay. On one occasion he retired a day's march from Phraaspa with ten legions, three praetorian cohorts and all of his cavalry systematically to despoil the surrounding countryside. Having drawn off a substantial Parthian force, Antony feinted leading his men back to their siege lines; in fact, he had given orders that his cavalry should charge as soon as the legions advanced near enough to support them. The Parthian horse shadowing his movements would not stand and fight, however; and though Antony's infantry pursued them for 10km and his cavalry for 20km more, they had nothing to show for it beyond 30 prisoners taken and only 80 Parthian dead. Returning to Phraaspa the following day, Antony had to fight his way through the main body of the Parthian army, which subjected him to incessant harassment.

Having reached the security of his camp, Antony discovered the cohorts left behind to maintain the investment of the city had panicked and fled when the garrison had sallied against the mound, putting his improvised siege machines to the torch. He restored discipline by decimating the offending units and putting the survivors on barley instead of wheat rations.

By October, Antony, subjected to periodic sorties by the besieged garrison and incessant raids on his increasingly far-flung foraging parties by Parthian horse archers, was forced to accept the reality that his campaign had failed. He broke camp with his men deployed in a hollow square, the baggage in the centre, lacing the intervals in the flanks and rear of his line of march with slingers and lightly armed troops, and giving orders to his horse to charge and drive off the enemy as they closed, but not to follow them far as they retired. These measures minimized his losses for the first four days of the retreat, but on the fifth day, Flavius Gallus, a senior officer, detached some light infantry and cavalry and held his ground, refusing to fall back upon the main force even when the quaestor Marcus Titius seized the standards and reversed them as the signal to withdraw, upbraiding Gallus for leading so many brave men to their destruction. Compounding this error, when Gallus was, inevitably, cut off and surrounded, Antony's subordinates dispatched covering forces piecemeal and in inadequate numbers to his aid. By their bad management the rout would have spread through the whole army if Antony himself had not marched from the van to both rally the fugitives and face down the Parthians, deterring them from any further pursuit. Antony lost 3,000 killed in this engagement, 5,000 more being carried back to the camp wounded, among them Gallus; shot through the body with four arrows, he subsequently died.

Sensing their advantage, the Parthians, their ranks swollen by reinforcements, including the royal bodyguard, spent the night near Antony's camp, in expectation of looting his tents and baggage, which they anticipated being abandoned. Roman discipline held, however, and the next morning the Parthians, convinced they were riding in to plunder rather than fight, were taken aback when they were received with a shower of missiles. The lightly armed troops then withdrew between the intervals of the legions, which closed up in a *testudo* of overlapping shields, immune to arrows and able to repulse enemy incursions at close quarters.

The Parthians subsequently reverted to their harassing tactics and avoided set-piece engagements. For the Roman, the situation worsened as famine and illness began to bite. The Parthians blocked the passes on the Roman line of retreat with trenches or palisades, poisoned the wells and destroyed the pasturage. The legionaries could find little food by foraging and besides this, with the few remaining baggage horses committed to carrying the sick and wounded, they had been forced to abandon their household implements, including the stone mortar and pestles used to grind wheat and make bread. Provisions ran so short that a barley loaf sold for its weight in silver. Surrender, however, was not an option. By shooting down those who attempted to desert, the Parthians sent a clear signal that no quarter would be offered.

Desperate to shake off the pursuit, Antony resorted to a succession of night marches that finally pushed his men too far. They began to run wild, killing those suspected to have any money, and ransacking the baggage, including Antony's personal goods, breaking his plate and dividing the fragments among

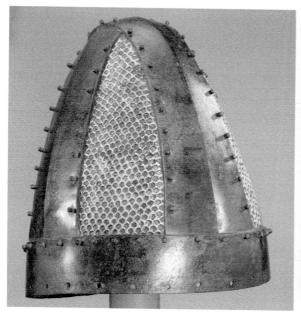

themselves. Assuming the commotion was the enemy inside the gates, Antony lost heart and contemplated suicide but pulled himself together just in time to quell the disturbances. With order barely restored, day began to break, and with it the renewed Parthian assault. Once again the lightly armed troops were ordered out to screen the rearguard as the fighting retreat continued. Having finally reached the Araxes, the last major river obstructing his line of march, Antony, drawing up the cavalry on the banks to keep the enemy at bay, first passed over the sick and wounded and then got the rest of the army across. The Parthians unstrung their bows as a mark of respect as the Romans crossed back into Armenia.

Over the 27 days since abandoning the siege of Phraaspa the Romans had survived 18 separate engagements with the enemy. Antony had nothing to show for it; in addition to almost all of his baggage, he had lost over one-third of one of the finest armies ever assembled in antiquity, over 40,000 men in all, equivalent to the entire force Crassus led to its doom at Carrhae.

Desperate to save face with something positive to justify this nightmarish debacle, Antony seized Artavasdes II of Armenia, shipped him off as a prisoner to Egypt and took control of Armenia in the spring of 35 BC, reducing it to the status of a Roman province. He marched into Media again in 34 BC, but his progress was bitterly contested by the combined actions of the Parthians and Armenians, the latter now taking a far more aggressive stance against the Romans after the abduction of their king. When Antony pulled his legions out of Armenia, mustering them for the confrontation with Octavian, Artaxias II (r. 34–20 BC), the son of Artavasdes II of Armenia, regained control of the country, massacring any Romans left behind. By the end of the decade Antony had lost first the battle of Actium on 2 September 31 BC and then his life when he committed suicide, dying in Cleopatra's arms in Alexandria, Egypt on 1 August 30 BC. His rival, Octavian, assumed power as the first emperor of Rome, Augustus (r. 27 BC– AD 14).

ABOVE LEFT
A helmet of the style worn by the Parthians, well-sloped to deflect downward blows. Parthian cataphracts seem to have ridden with the head protected but the face uncovered; their Sasanian successors progressed to a completely enclosed variant, sacrificing some vision for greater protection. (The Metropolitan Museum of Art, New York: Rogers Fund, 1962)

ABOVE RIGHT
Compared to his squat, bulbous visage as depicted on coins, this bust of Mark Antony (now in the Vatican Museum, Rome) represents a highly stylized portrait. The failure of Antony's Parthian campaign in 36 BC destroyed the reputation he had maintained since the battle of Philippi in 42 BC of being Rome's foremost warlord, cost him tens of thousands of irreplaceable veteran troops, and drove him into the arms of Cleopatra, all of which his rival, the wily Octavian, could twist to his advantage. (Bettmann/Getty Images)

Phraaspa to Nisibis

Civil war in Parthia between Phraates IV and Tiridates II afforded the Emperor Augustus an opportunity to settle the frontier in the East. After Tiridates II was defeated, he took refuge in Roman Syria, giving Augustus a valuable bargaining chip. In exchange for peace, in 23 BC Phraates IV conceded Roman hegemony over Armenia, handed over five of his sons as hostages and returned Roman prisoners of war, along with their legionary standards.

In all respects but one, the settlement of Augustus offered the basis for Roman/Parthian rapprochement. The blind spot was Armenia, where each succession to the throne created a crisis that threatened to draw in both superpowers. After the assassination of Orodes III in AD 6, Augustus endorsed Vonones, eldest son of Phraates IV, as the new King of Parthia. After Vonones I was overthrown by Arsaces XXVIII, King of Media Atropatene, who assumed power in Parthia as Artabanus III (r. AD 10–40), the Emperor Tiberius installed Vonones I as King of Armenia in AD 8. This was unacceptable to Artabanus III, and the Romans backed down, replacing Vonones I with another candidate, Zeno.

Another crisis erupted in AD 35 when Artabanus III placed his son, Arsaces I, on the vacant Armenian throne. In response, the Romans induced the peoples of the Caucasus to occupy Armenia (and execute Arsaces I that same year) and then invade Parthia. The Romans themselves mobilized to cross the Euphrates while encouraging Tiridates III (r. AD 35–36), a grandson of Phraates IV, to seize power in Ctesiphon. Artabanus III won the ensuing civil war but renounced any right to intervene in Armenia.

Outright war erupted in AD 54, after Vologases I (r. AD 51–78) invaded Armenia in AD 52 and installed his brother as King Tiridates I of Armenia (r. AD 53–58 and 62–88). The Emperor Nero (r. AD 54–68) ordered Gnaeus Domitius Corbulo to resolve the situation. Of the four legions garrisoning Syria, two would remain in Syria, while two would advance into Armenia with Corbulo, supported by Rome's client kings in Chalcis and Commagene. After spending AD 55 and 56 readying the legions at his disposal, while adding a fifth to his command, at the end of AD 57 Corbulo advanced into Armenia, where he wintered at Carana.

The following year, Roman allies in the Caucasus exerted pressure on Armenia from the north while Vologases I, mired in a major insurrection, was unable to intervene. After taking the outlying forts, Corbulo seized Artaxata in AD 58 and Tigranocerta in AD 59. After installing Tigranes VI as Rome's client king of Armenia in AD 60 (r. AD 60–c.61/62), Corbulo returned to Syria.

The following year, Tigranes VI invaded Adiabene. Its king requested aid from Vologases I, who sent Parthian forces into Armenia and Syria. In response, Corbulo sent two legions to aid Tigranes VI and requested a field commander for the Armenian venture. In the event, the Romans were able to eject the Parthians from Armenia and hold the Euphrates. When Lucius Caesennius Paetus, Nero's selection for command in Armenia, arrived, Corbulo divided the six legions under his command, retaining three while Paetus received the others.

In AD 62, Paetus advanced to Tigranocerta with two legions, only to be outmanoeuvred by Vologases I, who wiped out the Roman garrisons holding the mountain passes, and shut Paetus up in Rhandeia, near the Arsanias River. Dio claims Vologases I was on the point of retiring, for he lacked siege engines and the provisions for a long siege (Dio VIII: 123). Broken psychologically, however, Paetus requested a truce and promised to withdraw from Armenia, which would revert to Tiridates I. Nero then handed Corbulo supreme military command in the East and authority over all Rome's client kings, plus an additional legion from Pannonia. In late AD 63, Corbulo and Vologases I negotiated a compromise settlement; in AD 66, Tiridates I received his crown from Nero's own hand, reflecting Rome's primacy.

Following this, relations between Rome and Parthia remained relatively peaceful for another 50 years. The Parthians stood by as Rome annexed its client kingdoms – Colchis and Pontus in AD 64, Commagene, Lesser Armenia and Cilicia in AD 72 – descended into near-anarchy during the Year of the Four Emperors in AD 69, and suppressed the Judean revolt in AD 70. After Vologases I died in AD 78, Parthia succumbed to a dynastic struggle that continued until the accession of Osroes I in AD 109. The following year, the King of Armenia died and Osroes I, who was contesting for the throne with a rival, Vologases III, opted to strengthen his position by replacing him with his nephew, Axidares (r. AD 110–113), without consulting Rome.

This provocation was poorly timed, as Rome was now ruled by an expansionist emperor, Trajan (r. AD 98–117). Interference in Armenia was just the pretext Trajan was looking for to settle accounts with the Parthians. Rome's eastern legions prepared for a major offensive; Trajan had more than 80,000 men mobilized in total. Osroes I deposed his nephew in a bid to placate Trajan, suggesting that the emperor revive the old arrangement by crowning Parthamasiris, Axidares' younger brother, as King of Armenia. Playing along, in AD 114 Trajan received Parthamasiris, who laid his crown at Trajan's feet, expecting the emperor to place it on his head. Instead, Trajan informed Parthamasiris that he had just forfeited the crown. Armenia was annexed as a Roman province and its monarchy abolished.

In AD 115, Trajan annexed another province, Mesopotamia. After spending the winter of AD 115/116 in Antioch, he advanced to the Tigris, where he split his army in two: one division took Adenystrae (modern-day Mardin) without a fight, while the second advanced to Dura-Europos, where it would link up with a supply fleet and then proceed down the east bank of the Euphrates until reaching Babylon. Trajan then had the fleet ported overland from the Euphrates to the Tigris, from where he took Seleucia and then Ctesiphon unopposed. The Roman fleet then sailed down the Tigris to Charax (modern-day Basra). Rome was at its territorial apogee, but these achievements left the Romans grossly over-extended. Osroes I remained at large, and everywhere along a 965km front the Parthians were able to harass the invaders. Roman supply lines were dangerously exposed, and the key city of Hatra became a focus of resistance.

Revolts erupted throughout Mesopotamia, the Roman garrisons at Seleucia on the Euphrates, Nisibis (modern-day Nusaybin) and Edessa (modern-day Urfa) being evicted by the local populations. Trajan sent three divisions to quash the rebellion. One force was defeated, and its commander slain; the second force recovered Nisibis and Edessa; the third force recaptured Seleucia. Trajan recognized the strategic limitations of his position when he crowned Parthamaspates, a son of Osroes I, as his client king of Parthia. This failed to satisfy Parthian nationalism, and Trajan himself failed to take Hatra. He lifted the siege and withdrew, intending to return to Rome but dying en route on 8 August AD 117.

Trajan's successor, Hadrian (r. AD 117–138), promptly reversed his predecessor's policy. He re-established the Euphrates as the frontier, conceding Mesopotamia back to Parthia and Adiabene back to its ruling dynasty. Bereft of Roman support, Parthamaspates (r. AD 116) was quickly defeated by Osroes I, who reclaimed the throne. Hadrian subsequently installed Parthamaspates as King of Osrhoene. He also recognized Vologases III, another rival to Osroes I, as the new King of Armenia, guaranteeing that Parthia would be rent by civil war to AD 147.

When Vologases IV (r. AD 147–191) received word of the death of Antoninus Pius (r. AD 138–161) in AD 161 he entered Armenia, expelled King Gaius Julius Sohaemus (r. AD 144–161) and replaced him with an Arsacid prince, Pacorus (r. AD 161–164). Marcus Sedatius Severianus, the governor of Cappadocia, advanced into Armenia, but was surprised by the Parthians on the march and forced to take shelter in Elegeia. After three days the Roman force was wiped out, Severianus committing suicide. Vologases IV crossed the Euphrates and defeated Lucius Attidius Cornelianus, the governor of Syria, overrunning Osrhoene and imposing a client king, Vaël, on Edessa.

With conditions in the East becoming critical, Marcus Aurelius (r. AD 161–180) stripped the northern frontiers to the bone in order to assemble the force necessary to stabilize the situation. In addition to three full legions, detachments from four or five more were mobilized. Ostensibly, co-Emperor Lucius was in overall command – but soon side-lined owing to his unsuitability – with the support of generals Avidius Cassius, Statius Priscus, Julius Severus, Publius Martius Verus and Marcus Claudius Fronto. Priscus, with two legions, entered Armenia in the spring of AD 163, seized the capital, Artaxata, and reinstated Sohaemus as king (r. AD 163–c.186). Meanwhile, the Parthians invaded Osrhoene, entered Edessa, and replaced the pro-Roman ruler with a Parthian vassal. The Romans responded by sending a force along the Roman side of the Euphrates to defeat the Parthians at Sura. The recovery of Sura allowed the Romans to occupy the fortresses of Dausara and Nicephorium on the northern bank of the Euphrates. Fronto pushed into Osrhoene from Armenia, securing the border with Syria. The Romans spent AD 164 mopping up the remaining Parthian detachments in Syria and preparing for a decisive offensive.

In AD 165, two Roman columns struck across the Euphrates. The northern column, under Verus, retook Edessa and reinstated the pro-Roman king before driving eastwards to capture Nisibis. Meanwhile, Avidius advanced down the Euphrates and defeated the Parthians at Dura-Europos. This opened up Mesopotamia to invasion, and Avidius pushed south to attack Seleucia and Ctesiphon on the Tigris. Seleucia surrendered on terms, but the armistice did not hold and the city was sacked and burned. Avidius then stormed and plundered Ctesiphon. Syria was enlarged to include Dura-Europos, which now marked Rome's southern frontier in Mesopotamia; Nisibis became the crux of the Roman presence in upper Mesopotamia. Aurelius was awarded the title *Parthicus Maximus* ('Great Victor in Parthia') by the Senate, but the plague brought back to the empire by the returning Roman forces would devastate the Mediterranean world; the death toll ran into the millions.

Seeking to take advantage of the civil war between Septimius Severus and Pescennius Niger that erupted in Rome after the assassination of the Emperor Commodus (r. AD 180–192) in AD 192, Vologases V (r. AD 191–208) incited Osrhoene to rebel and ordered Adiabene and Osrhoene to besiege Nisibis. Late in the spring of AD 195, the Emperor Septimius Severus (r. AD 193–211) crossed the Euphrates, forced Osrhoene's capitulation and advanced to Nisibis. Severus had to return west to deal with another rival, Clodius Albinus; in the emperor's absence, his lieutenants seized Adiabene. Vologases V failed to capture Nisibis, but retook Adiabene.

In AD 197, using the friendship shown to Niger by Abdsamiya, King of Hatra (r. AD 180–205), as his pretext, Severus returned to the fray, raising three new legions – increasing the total size of the Army from perhaps 375,000 to 450,000 men – and fielding two columns in his offensive against Parthia. The kings of Armenia and Osrhoene bought peace by offering pacts, gifts, hostages and auxiliaries. Severus marched via Adiabene into Arabia Felix, heading for Hatra. Although Severus pressed the siege of the city vigorously, resistance was fierce and the emperor finally broke off, electing to march south into lower Mesopotamia. The Parthians retreated, abandoning Babylon and Seleucia. On 28 January AD 198 the Romans stormed Ctesiphon, Vologases V fleeing while the Romans plundered his treasury. Severus could be satisfied with the outcome of the campaign; the Senate awarded him the title *Parthicus Maximus*. Two of the three new legions, I *Parthica* and III *Parthica*, were stationed in the new province of Mesopotamia.

Nisibis

AD 217

BACKGROUND TO BATTLE

Vologases V died in AD 208. His two sons, Vologases VI and Artabanus V, then warred for the throne. When the Emperor Septimius Severus died in AD 211, he was succeeded by the joint rule of his sons Caracalla and Geta – an unwieldy arrangement that ended with the assassination of the latter by the former before the year was out. Caracalla, who aspired to fulfil the legacy of Alexander the Great, then assembled a powerful invasion force, which set out for the Parthian frontier after spending the winter of AD 213/14 mustering at Nicomedia (modern-day İzmit). This army included the imperial Horse Guards (*Equites Singulares Augusti*) and ten cohorts of the Praetorian Guard; legions II *Parthica*, II *Adriutrix* and XXX *Ulpia*; detachments from legions III *Augusta*, III *Gallica*, IV *Falvia*, XIII and XIV *Gemina*; and auxiliaries, including Caracalla's personal project, a Macedonian-style phalanx – 16,000 strong, according to Dio (Dio IX: 293) – and a *lochos* (cohort) dubbed the Spartans. In addition to their names evoking the exploits of Alexander, whose Greek army had conquered Persia, these units reflected real forward thinking by Caracalla. Units in the phalanx were equipped with long spears, the massed bristling points of which would empower infantry to hold their ground against cavalry on an open plain. The Spartans were equipped with clubs, blunt-force weapons that could stun and disable the heavily armoured cataphracts in a way pointed and bladed weapons could not.

After a diversion to Alexandria in AD 215, the population of which was subjected to a salutary massacre when Caracalla, for unknown reasons, unleashed his troops on the city, the Roman force pushed on to the East. Even with this imminent threat bearing down, Parthia remained divided between Artabanus V (r. AD 213–224), backed by the Karins, Andigan, Kanarangiya,

This bust of the Emperor Caracalla hints at his severity and cruelty. Although notorious for his amorality in the pursuit of power (which extended to the assassination of his brother and the execution of his wife) and savagery in the exercise of power (which included the wholesale massacre of the citizens of Alexandria), Caracalla was responsible for both major investments in public infrastructure (e.g. the baths that bear his name) and constitutional reform; it was he who granted Roman citizenship to all free men within the empire. Ruthless and driven to emulate the achievements of his idol, Alexander the Great, Caracalla was poised to unleash the full power of the Roman war machine against the East at the moment of his death in AD 217. No-one benefited more from his assassination than the Parthians. (DEA/G. DAGLI ORTI/De Agostini via Getty Images)

Jusnafs and Ziks, and Vologases VI (r. AD 208–228), supported by the Suren, Mihran, Spandiyadh and Ispahbudhan. Meanwhile, a new house, the Sasanian, was beginning its rise in the province of Fars.

While the Parthians turned on each other, Caracalla established his headquarters at Antioch in the summer of AD 215 and began to consolidate control over the eastern buffer states. Colonial status was awarded to Antioch and Emesa (modern-day Homs), possibly to Palmyra (if not already under the Emperor Septimius Severus), and to Edessa (modern-day Urfa), the former capital of the kingdom of Osrhoene that was now incorporated into the provincial structure, its last king, Abgarus IX (r. AD 177–212), having been seized when lured to the camp of Caracalla under the pretext of negotiations. When Caracalla employed the same ruse against Khosrov I of Armenia (r. AD 198–217), that country rose in rebellion; its king remained in Roman hands until his death in AD 217, at which point his son, Tiridates II (r. AD 217–252), was granted the crown by Caracalla.

In AD 216, Caracalla had approached Artabanus V with an unprecedented offer; to unite their dynasties – and empires – by marrying one of the

The tombstone of a Roman soldier who served and died in Londinium, Britannia. He is wearing a tunic fastened at the waist, which is partially covered by a *caracalla* (cloak) that is buttoned at the top. The Emperor Caracalla (r. AD 198–217), who had a tendency to favour northern European styles, became so associated with this item of clothing that he is remembered by history in its name. (Museum of London/Heritage Images/Getty Images)

king's daughters (the emperor was a widower; having been forced into an arranged marriage by his father, he had disposed of his wife, Fulvia Plautilla, as soon as Severus was dead). Caracalla pointed out that the Roman and the Parthian empires were the largest in the world; if they were united by marriage, the nations outside their authority could easily be reduced, as the Roman infantry were invincible in close-quarters combat, and the Parthian cavalry was without peer. The two forces complemented each other; by waging war together, they could easily unite the entire inhabited world under a single crown. Economic benefits would also flow from this political union, Parthian spices and textiles exchanging freely with Roman metals and manufactured goods in a common market. Artabanus V at first demurred, insisting it was not appropriate for a Parthian to marry a Roman because through the offspring of such a union the bloodlines of both races would be rendered impure (Herodian 4.10.5). He was finally won over, however, and Caracalla crossed the Euphrates unopposed to rendezvous with his future bride and father-in-law.

The reception, held outdoors, was quite a spectacle. The elite of Parthian society were in attendance, crowned with the traditional flowers and clad in sumptuous ceremonial dress embroidered with gold and bright colours for the occasion. As the wine continued to flow, the Parthians began dancing, accompanied by the piping of flutes and the pounding of drums. Caracalla was aware that, as Herodian recorded, it was characteristic of the Parthians to party hard, and drink hard, on such occasions (Herodian 4.11.3). The emperor waited until the right moment before giving a prearranged signal, whereupon his troops proceeded to slaughter the entire wedding party. The Parthians, having somehow allowed the Romans to smuggle arms into the reception, were themselves defenceless, having left their bows and quivers with their mounts, not having anticipated needing their weapons at a wedding (Herodian 4.11.7). Artabanus V, helped onto a horse by some of his personal bodyguards, barely escaped with a few companions. The rest of the Parthians, who had sent their horses out to graze, were massacred as they vainly sought to flee on foot, hindered by the long, loose robes of their banquet attire (Herodian 4.11.6). There is no reference to the ultimate fate of Caracalla's unfortunate second wife; presumably, she went the way of the first.

After butchering as much of the Parthian elite as he could catch, and taking much booty and many prisoners, Caracalla debauched his way through the Parthian heartland, pillaging and burning. When he captured Arbela (modern-day Erbil) in AD 216, he desecrated the royal tombs of the Parthian kings, scattering their bones. Finally, he and his troops, burdened by the loot they had accumulated, withdrew to Syria (Herodian 4.11.8).

Enraged, Artabanus V spent the winter sending out summons' to every satrap in the Parthian Empire to assemble with their retainers for a counter-attack the following campaign season. When spring AD 217 came, Caracalla advanced towards Edessa. On 8 April, outside of Carrhae, he decided to relieve himself prior to visiting the oracle at the Temple of the Moon. Caracalla ordered his escort to move along, as he wanted some privacy, but one of his bodyguards broke ranks to stab the emperor in the back, killing him.

The imperial army, about to go toe-to-toe with an enemy thirsting for revenge, needed a new emperor. By consensus among the officers, the choice fell on Marcus Opellius Macrinus, a prefect of the Praetorian Guard. It was a curious decision, given the widespread assumption that Macrinus had instigated the assassination of his predecessor. He was certainly not the choice of the rank and file, who had respected Caracalla and anticipated a tough fight to come, for Artabanus V was fast approaching with a massive army, while Macrinus was a bureaucrat and legal functionary with no military background. Indeed, the first instinct of the new emperor (r. AD 217–218) was to be conciliatory: he released Parthian captives to Artabanus V with a friendly greeting, urging him to accept peace. Artabanus V refused to entertain this proposal, however, unless the Romans pledged to abandon Mesopotamia entirely, rebuild the forts and cities they had demolished, and make reparations for the desecration inflicted on the royal tombs.

The two armies camped opposite each other at Nisibis (modern-day Nusaybin, on the Turkey/Syria border). The Parthians were clearly spoiling for a fight; the Romans were worsted in a skirmish between foraging parties over the water supply.

Macrinus had no option other than to offer a pitched battle. Herodian recounts that this was preceded by his giving a less-than-inspiring pep talk to his army in which he conceded that the Parthians were entirely justified in their rage, for it was the Romans who had incited the conflict by an unprovoked breach of treaty complemented by mass murder and desecration (Herodian 4.14.6). The ethics of the coming struggle, however, were ultimately irrelevant. Macrinus was careful to remind his men that, as professional soldiers, they would have the advantage over the Parthians, whose inherent decentralization would prove to be their ultimate undoing. By standing firm, he told them, the Romans would wear down the enemy until, their passion spent, they withdrew from the field. Therefore, he urged them, fight in the spirit of your forebears; superior logistics, superior tactics, and above all, superior discipline would carry the day.

A Parthian sword. This appears to be the shorter type, dubbed the *akinakes*. The Emperor Caracalla kept many pet lions; his favourite was named after this weapon. (© akg-images/ Dr. Uwe Ellerbrock)

1 The Parthians form a front line of five divisions, with a reserve in the rear. Each division is comprised of mounted archers surrounding a core of cataphract heavy cavalry. Camel cataphracts are deployed on the flanks to disrupt the Roman cavalry opposite.

2 The Romans form up with the legions in the centre screened by light infantry. Roman and auxiliary cavalry supported by missile troops are stationed on the left and right flanks to prevent the Parthians from outflanking or encircling the infantry.

3 The Parthians initiate combat at dawn on the first day. Loosing arrows all the while, the horse archers first ride towards the Romans, then break parallel to their front line before returning to their baggage train to restock their quivers, units alternating through this cycle to keep the Romans under a constant hail of missiles.

4 As the cataphracts charge, the Roman light infantry fall back through the lanes left open by the legions, scattering caltrops behind them as they withdraw. The cataphracts, especially the camels, are hampered by these obstacles and are unable to break the Roman line. The Parthians seek to outflank the Romans on both wings. The Romans deploy their reserves to lengthen their line.

5 On the second day, the Parthians again seek to outflank the Romans on both wings. The Romans again deploy their reserves to lengthen their line.

6 On the third day, the Parthians finally succeed in overlapping the Roman line.

7 The Roman legions are only saved from being encircled by the non-combatants of their camp, who sortie out and catch the Parthians unawares. Both sides are now exhausted and agree to settle on terms.

Battlefield environment

The last clash between the Roman and Parthian empires was not on a ground of Roman choosing. Nisibis (modern-day Nusaybin) was a prosperous city that straddled the border between the two regional superpowers and had changed hands multiple times throughout the endemic conflicts between Rome and Parthia, most recently reverting to Roman authority when it had been occupied by Septimius Severus in AD 197. His son and successor, Caracalla, had sought to build on this legacy, campaigning successfully (if treacherously) in the East throughout AD 216. His objectives for the next phase of the war will never be known, for he was assassinated at Carrhae on 8 April of the following year. The army was left without a commander-in-chief for the next three days as the high command wrangled over who would succeed to the role. By the time Macrinus emerged as the new emperor, a vengeful Parthian host had descended on the Roman position. Macrinus was unwilling to risk withdrawing across open country, which would leave the army exposed on the march to the hit-and-run tactics at which the Parthians excelled. Nor could he garrison the army inside Nisibis in order to wait the enemy out; while the Parthians lacked siege craft, the Roman forces were too numerous, and the city too small, for it to sustain them. With no other option, Macrinus drew his legions up in battle array, a challenge the Parthians, burning for revenge after the desecration of their heartland, were only too willing to accept.

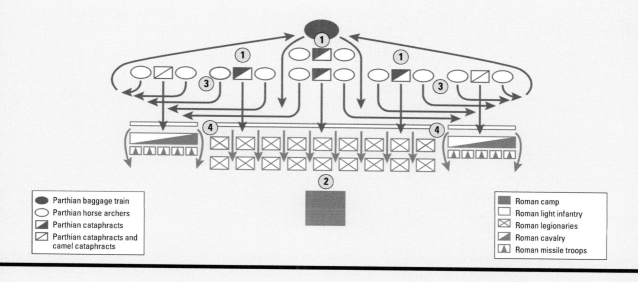

Parthian baggage train
Parthian horse archers
Parthian cataphracts
Parthian cataphracts and camel cataphracts

Roman camp
Roman light infantry
Roman legionaries
Roman cavalry
Roman missile troops

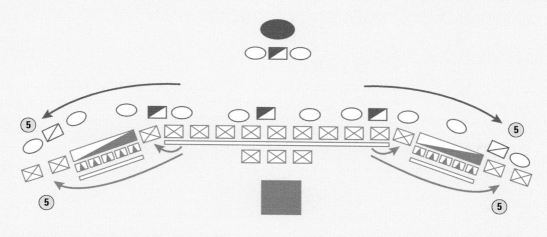

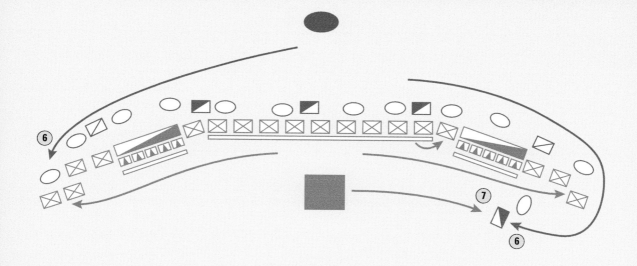

Nusaybin (ancient Nisibis) was a frontier town in antiquity, straddling the border between East and West. It retains that distinction today, lying just inside Turkey on its southern border, facing Syria. As the heavy security suggests, frontier conditions today are as unsettled as they were in AD 217, when Roman and Parthian forces squared off against each other in this vicinity for their last set-piece battle. (Andia/Universal Images Group via Getty Images)

INTO COMBAT

In the dim light of dawn just before sunrise the following morning, both armies began to assemble into battle formations. Macrinus placed his legions in the centre, with lanes left open to allow light infantry to deploy at the front or rear as necessary. Interspersed with the Roman infantry were missile units, including slingers and archers. Roman and auxiliary cavalry, including specialist Moorish javelin-throwing light cavalry, were stationed on the left and right flanks to prevent the Parthian cataphracts or horse archers from outflanking or encircling them.

In addition to the standard horse-archer and cataphract cavalry, Artabanus V incorporated a new unit, making its combat debut in this battle: cataphract camels, possibly ridden by Arabs rather than Parthians. The Parthian army would have manifested its standard patchwork agglomeration of semi-autonomous divisions comprising the personal retinues mobilized by the great houses, each of which was divided into wings consisting of mounted archers surrounding a core of cataphracts. Artabanus V would have been counting on the renowned aversion of horses towards camels to offer a tactical advantage, so in all likelihood the camels were deployed in the front ranks of the Parthian divisions to disorder the Roman cavalry formation just before the units engaged.

At dawn, having hailed the rising sun, as was their custom, the Parthians, with a deafening roar, opened the battle by charging the Roman line, loosing their arrows and whipping on their horses. The showers of Parthian arrows inflicted considerable injury, as did the long spears of the heavy cavalry. The well-drilled Roman legions stood their ground, however, maintaining an unbroken shield wall while cycling fresh cohorts into the front line from their reserves. The Roman light infantry, meanwhile, employed a tactical initiative of its own to take the sting out of the cataphract threat. Advancing ahead of the shield wall so as to invite a charge by the enemy, they would then feign a retreat, dropping caltrops behind them as they pulled back. Covered by the sand, these spiked obstacles were invisible to the Parthian cavalry; as the horses, and particularly the tender-footed dromedaries, trod on these implements they bucked and fell in their anguish, throwing their riders. For so long as he remained on horseback the Parthian was a formidable adversary, Herodian conceded, but if he dismounted or was thrown from the saddle, he was effectively neutralized, as he was no match for a legionary in hand-to-hand fighting (Herodian 4.15.3).

On the first and second days the two armies grappled from morning until evening, and when night put an end to the fighting, each side withdrew to its own camp, claiming the victory. With brute force having failed to break the enemy, on the third day the Parthians sought to utilize their superior numbers by outflanking the Roman lines. Alerted to this threat, Macrinus was forced to sacrifice the depth of his army in favour of its length. By committing the reserves from his second line to his ever-widening wings he broadened his front in order to counter every Parthian attempt at encirclement.

However, the Romans were being worn down by the relentless attacks of the Parthians and could extend their lines to avoid being outflanked for only so long against an enemy who had both greater mobility and numerical superiority. Finally, on one or both flanks, the Romans were overlapped. The Parthians now had the opportunity to strike their foe in the rear. It was the tipping point of the battle; Macrinus was only saved by his non-combatant drivers, shield-bearers and baggage handlers, who charged out of the army's fortified camp, taking the Parthians by surprise. Ironically, the Parthians may have let the advantage here slip through their fingers because they accorded the Romans too much respect. The appearance of fresh Roman troops from this unexpected quarter, just when the balance of the battle seemed to have tipped their way, must have convinced the Parthians that they had been lured into a trap, a pre-planned Roman manoeuvre to crush them between the camp and the main body of the army.

The ghost of Caracalla thus gained one last victory, for the first instinct of the Parthians, still unaware of his assassination, was to assume that he had unleashed one of his characteristically duplicitous tactical gambits. They would never have credited Macrinus with having such foresight or cold-blooded nerve, and indeed, he had nothing to do with it. The sortie was a spontaneous and desperate gamble; had the Parthians realized that they were being challenged not by front-line troops but by a motley collection of walking wounded and service personnel, these might have been swiftly overwhelmed, leaving the Parthians free to storm the camp's open gates and unguarded walls. In the short term, the Romans might have survived being surrounded by wheeling about the rearmost cohorts of their line to form a new perimeter, but that night they would have been forced to remain on the battlefield. Cut off from water and shelter, his camp occupied and plundered, Macrinus would have had no choice but to surrender his entire army on Parthian terms the next day.

The quick-thinking camp prefect responsible for this initiative had saved the day, but the killing raged on. Herodian's vivid description captures the horrific intensity of the struggle as the battle reached its climax; his account

The route by which Macrinus (r. AD 217–218) became emperor was as circuitous as his ultimate ascension was unlikely. By origin a Berber from Mauretania in Roman northern Africa, he became the first emperor from outside the senatorial class, having risen no higher than the equestrian. He served Caracalla as a praetorian prefect, but his forte was legal and civil administrative affairs, and he had no military background. He accompanied Caracalla on his Parthian campaign and succeeded, in highly suspicious circumstances, following his predecessor's assassination on 8 April AD 217. His generalship was found wanting at Nisibis, and the huge indemnity he was subsequently forced to pay cost him whatever support he ever commanded. Macrinus was not destined to reign for long. (Noble Numismatics, https://www.noble.com.au/)

Nisibis, AD 217

As the sun set on the third day of the Battle of Nisibis, both sides remained locked together, grappling to the end as the last rays of light settled over the featureless plain that so many thousands had already lost their lives contesting. As Parthian horse archers continue to cruise the field, saturating the Roman ranks with an incessant hail of arrows, wave after wave of Parthian heavy cavalry – the cataphracts – crash into the Roman front line. Both rider and horse, encased in iron from head to toe, are largely immune to edged weapons, even the penetrative point of the *pilum*. Each mounted warrior wields a long lance, the *kontos*, and seeks to pierce the body armour worn by each legionary to land a killing blow from outside the cutting arc of the Roman swords.

The Romans fought back with everything in their arsenal. While blades were of limited use, the heavily armoured Parthians were vulnerable to blunt-force weapons – sling stones at long range, clubs at close quarters. To take the sting out of the enemy's charge, the Romans scattered caltrops across the field to discomfit the Parthian mounts. This was especially effective against the new Parthian cavalry corps, composed of camel-riding cataphracts. Whenever their soft, padded feet trod on the barbed point of a caltrop the beasts would contort in agony, throwing their riders and bolting wildly up and down the line.

speaks of the entire plain being carpeted by the bodies of the dead and dying, beasts as well as men, to the extent that the surface of the earth itself could no longer be made out (Herodian 4.15.5). Where the fighting was heaviest, corpses were piled up in huge mounds. Apparently, the camels did not turn out to be the wonder weapon the Parthians had hoped for; they especially fell in heaps where they were slain. Ultimately, ironically, the very profligate extremity of the slaughter forced an end to the killing. The front line became

A full coat of horse armour, excavated from Dura-Europos and modelled intact on a live mount. This set belonged to the Roman garrison. Well before the mid-3rd century AD, from which this example dates, the Romans had been steadily up-armouring their own cavalry, in addition to hiring auxiliary cavalry from peoples who boasted their own line of cataphracts, such as the Armenians and Sarmatians, in a bid to match the Parthians with something at least close to parity. (Yale University)

so congested with those who had fallen that those who remained alive could no longer come to blows. With their cataphracts unable to close with the foe across such a congested field, and their archers unable to pick out targets behind such macabre impromptu barricades, the Parthians pulled back to their camp, leaving the Romans free to do the same. As night fell, the clamour of battle – the clash of steel and the thunder of hooves, the shrill of horns and the beating of drums, the guttural shouting of war cries and the hoarse barking of orders – all faded until all that was left was the cacophony of agonized human and animal screams echoing in the darkness from the forsaken wounded.

Both sides were exhausted, but the Parthians showed no sign of breaking off the engagement. Carrying their dead from the field and burying them that night, they were clearly intending to renew the conflict at dawn the next morning. Canvassing his options, Macrinus concluded that he could not risk a fourth day of battle. His lines had held – just – but they were stretched to breaking point; he had no more reserves available to secure his flanks, and he had no alternative to the reactive stance of standing his ground and offering the enemy a target for the next wave of assaults. He could not go over onto the offensive against a fleet-footed foe that would only welcome this opportunity to dance around and disrupt his formations as they advanced. In addition, there were political factors to consider. The legitimacy of his imperial title was extremely insecure; he was a long way from the centre of power in Rome; and his army, the sole basis for his authority, was in imminent danger of being ground down to irrelevance in a battle that could at best only culminate in the most pyrrhic of victories. It was time to return to the bargaining table.

Macrinus surmised that Artabanus V was making so strong a stand and battling so fiercely because he thought he was fighting against – and avenging himself on – Caracalla. He therefore sent an embassy to the Parthian king with a letter informing him that the emperor who had wronged him by breaking his treaties and violating his oaths was dead, having paid a richly deserved penalty for his crimes. He assured Artabanus V that he did not approve of Caracalla's actions, and promised to return any remaining captives and loot, plus pay reparations of 50 million *denarii*, in order to end the bloodshed. According to Dio, Artabanus V accepted the offer – on essentially the same terms Macrinus had proffered before the battle began – because in truth, the Parthians were restless after spending a prolonged period away from their homes and food was running short (Dio IX: 403).

On this ambiguous note – a drawn battle, in which both sides had applied the same tactics and exhibited the same strengths and vulnerabilities as in their every other encounter over the past two-and-a-half centuries – conflict between Rome and Parthia concluded. Macrinus and Artabanus V appear to have departed the battlefield on quite friendly terms. They would never meet again. Macrinus had a powerful enemy in Caracalla's aunt, Julia Maesa, who instigated a revolt in favour of her 14-year-old grandson, Elagabalus, as emperor (r. AD 218–222). Defeated at the battle of Antioch on 8 June AD 218, Macrinus was hunted down and executed in the aftermath. Artabanus V, last of the Parthian kings, was killed in battle with the Sasanians on 28 April AD 224; the victor took the throne as Ardashir I (r. AD 224–242), and it was his dynasty that would rule from Ctesiphon for the next 400 years.

Diadumenian was only eight years old when he was elevated to the role of Caesar by his father, the Emperor Macrinus, in May AD 217. He became co-emperor the following year when his father promoted him to Augustus. The circumstances, however, were far from propitious. Given that he was already under a cloud of suspicion for having masterminded the assassination of his predecessor Caracalla, his withdrawal following the bloody stalemate at Nisibis, coupled with payment of a massive indemnity to Parthia, had cost Macrinus whatever respect he might have commanded. A revolt broke out in May AD 218, inspired by Caracalla's aunt, Julia Maesa, in the name of her 14-year-old grandson Elagabalus. Macrinus was defeated at the battle of Antioch on 8 June AD 218; while he fled north to the Bosporus, he sent Diadumenian east to seek asylum in Parthia at the court of Artabanus V. Macrinus was captured on 8 June in Chalcedon and subsequently executed in Cappadocia, while Diadumenian was intercepted that same day at Zeugma and beheaded in late June. (Classic Numismatic Group, https://www.cngcoins.com/)

Analysis

Victory in battle goes to the side that has best integrated the three 'T's of warfare – tactics, technology and terrain – into its military doctrine. At Carrhae, this proved decisively to be the Parthians, who conclusively asserted their self-determination in the face of Roman imperial aggression by playing to their natural strengths in warfare: tactics (combined-arms light and heavy cavalry), technology (the composite bow) and terrain (flat, open country). Eurocentric commentators might maintain that the defeat of Crassus did not lessen the primacy of Western arms (Hanson 2002: 12), but in actuality, the catastrophe at Carrhae had profound implications. The Parthians were the first people in history to fight Rome to a standstill; they were the ones who, in the words of the historian Justinus, 'having divided the world, as it were, with the Romans' (Justinus XLI: i), forced Rome to accept the limits of power.

The confrontation between these two superpowers could superficially be read as analogous to the stand-off between the United States and the Soviet Union during the Cold War. This parallel ultimately fails, however. Rome and Parthia did not represent an existential threat to one another; as they proved, time and again, neither could finish the other off. Nor was there any ideological high ground at stake in their wars, no missionary impulse or justification for the endless bloodshed in a sincere desire to make the world a genuinely better place. Ultimately, the only lesson both sides learned was not learning their lesson.

Rome was trapped in the logic of expansion for its own sake. Every frontier crossed, every rival eliminated, created both new threats and new opportunities that impelled the state ever onwards to the next horizon. The cut-throat world of republican politics, in which military glory was a prerequisite for career advancement, accelerated this privatized imperialism in a frenzy of empire building. The only aspect of this institutionalized aggression that changed after the principate superseded the republic was its centralization in the person of the emperor.

In this way, Rome became committed to a security perimeter that made confrontation with Parthia inescapable. Once Rome crossed the Aegean Sea and acquired territories in Asia Minor, it was inevitably drawn east into Armenia to control the strategic routes linking Asia Minor east to Iran and north across the Caucasus. The Roman highway in northern Asia Minor, guarded by the legionary fortress at Satala (modern-day Sadak), ran west to east across the plateau to the Armenian capital of Artaxata and on to Media Atropatene. The southern route running due east from the legionary base at Melitene crossed the Euphrates at the province of Sophene then branched into a south-eastern extension leading to Mesopotamia and a north-eastern extension that skirted Lake Van and connected with the northern route in Armenia. To protect these assets, Rome had to have control of the north–south passes at Dariel and Derbent into the Caucasus, and of the east–west passes from Mesopotamia to Armenia at Bitlis and Ergani. The stakes in who maintained control over Armenia, therefore, were enormous, and neither Rome nor Parthia was willing to concede this to the other. Awkward compromises over the nomination of client kings could at best maintain an uneasy peace that as often as not would break down upon the next succession. Neither side possessed the capacity to settle the issue once and for all by annexing and assimilating the Armenians, a people defined – to this day – by their unyielding commitment to self-determination. The spheres of influence of both empires thus remained in a permanent state of overlap, acceptable to neither. Tension would become friction, friction would spark war, and war would resolve nothing. There would be negotiation, compromise, settlement and then the tension of waiting for the inevitable next round of conflict would resume.

Wars between Rome and Parthia were one-sided in the sense that Rome was typically the aggressor and always relatively immune from reprisal. It is true that Syria, one of the richest provinces in the empire, was exposed to Parthian incursion from directly across the Euphrates. This necessitated a correspondingly large commitment of imperial manpower in its defence; in fact, after the accession of Augustus in 27 BC there were never fewer than four legions stationed there. These succeeded in holding the river crossings and containing the enemy for the next two-and-a-half centuries. The Parthians had only broken into Syria twice before that – in the wake of their victory at Carrhae in 53 BC, and while the republic was massively destabilized after Brutus and Cassius fell at the battle of Philippi in 42 BC. On both occasions, the Parthians were ultimately repulsed with heavy losses, their king losing his son and heir. Successive Parthian monarchs would elect to maintain a policy

The bloodless return by the Parthians of the Roman legionary standards lost at Carrhae represented a diplomatic triumph for the Emperor Augustus, one literally close to his heart. This larger-than-life Prima Porta statue portrays him standing barefoot with his right arm empty of a sword, raised in a gesture of peace. The centre of his breastplate depicts a Parthian offering the captured standards to a Roman officer (perhaps Tiberius). The restored standards were placed on display in a new monumental temple erected in Rome to honour the war god Mars Ultor (Mars the Avenger). (DEA PICTURE LIBRARY/ De Agostini via Getty Images)

Rome achieved the apogee of its military power and territorial extent under the Emperor Trajan. His campaigns conquered Dacia and Petra, reduced Armenia from a client state to a Roman province, and pushed all the way to the Persian Gulf after sacking Ctesiphon. While a triumph of planning and logistics, the Parthian campaign was ultimately doomed to failure. Rome lacked the manpower to garrison the provinces wrested from Parthia and the army was overstretched trying to stamp out the insurgencies that erupted in its wake. Trajan's successor, Hadrian (r. AD 117–138), was criticized by contemporaries for giving up Mesopotamia, but he had no choice other than to rationalize Rome's eastern frontier by withdrawing to a defensible line. (Classic Numismatic Group, https://www.cngcoins.com/)

The triumphal Arch of Septimius Severus, built in AD 203 in Rome, commemorates the Roman victory over Parthia, which culminated in the sack of Ctesiphon and the annexation of northern Mesopotamia. In these two images, Parthian prisoners of war are led into captivity. (Prisma/UIG/Getty Images)

of reactive as opposed to proactive force in relation to their arrogant and unwelcome neighbour.

The Arsacid dynasts appreciated that while they could ride and raid at will, they were in no position permanently to eliminate the Roman presence on their frontier. Even had they been able to muster the entire offensive potential of their empire, an invasion on such a scale would have foundered because of inadequate logistics, the variable terrain, networks of fortified 'hard-points' in the defence that would have to be bypassed because the Parthians lacked a siege train, and the fact that Rome's combined-arms approach to warfare would allow for multiple tactical options both in defence and in swinging over to the counter-attack. For these reasons, the Parthians were prepared to intervene in Armenia but not in Roman territory proper, not even when the opportunity presented itself through uprisings among the region's colonized peoples. For example, in AD 66, when Judea erupted in revolt, Parthia declined to offer support, even when imperial authority completely fragmented in a spasm of civil war during the Year of the Four Emperors in AD 69.

Throughout their rivalry, Rome enjoyed significant advantages over Parthia in political organization, military power and wealth. Parthia, therefore, could not hope to detach Roman territory on the periphery of the empire, let alone strike at Rome itself. The reverse was certainly not the case. The Parthians had advanced their capital to Ctesiphon in order to emphasize their hegemony over Mesopotamia, the bread basket and financial hub of their empire; but this left them horrifically exposed to Roman invasions that could march or boat straight down the Euphrates into the very core of their state. Rome in fact succeeded in sacking Ctesiphon on six separate occasions.

Rome was never able to consummate these victories through permanent annexation of the conquered territories, however. Fundamentally, this was because the Romans were never able to overcome the Parthian advantage in mobility. The deeper into Parthian space they advanced, the longer their lines of communication and supply were stretched, and the more vulnerable they became to interdiction by Parthian cavalry. The only viable countermeasure

to this threat was to station fortified garrisons along the route of march in order to retain the territory gained and protect the vital logistical chains. The longer this went on, however, the more units would have to be detached from the field force, which would ultimately be whittled down to the point where it was incapable of offensive action.

The inescapable fact was that Rome did not have the resources necessary to conquer and hold Mesopotamia east of the Euphrates, let alone the Persian heartland. Alexander the Great had done it; but his only commitment otherwise was Greece. The emperors were responsible for maintaining frontiers that stretched the length of the Rhine and Danube rivers and extended north to Hadrian's Wall and south to the desert fringe of the Sahara Desert. Conquering Parthia would have required the full commitment of the empire's entire military establishment, but concentrating this force on one enemy would have meant exposing the rest of the empire to a host of others. The emperors could not risk losing their existing provinces for the dubious prospect of incorporating more in a campaign that, even if successful at a tactical level on the battlefield, would have required years of commitment to pacification among the newly subjugated peoples. In the end, the Roman Empire, by inheriting Parthia's open and uncertain border onto Central Asia, would only have succeeded in being more over-extended than ever.

Parthian society was deeply conservative, and the feudal nature of its social structure made centrally directed reform anathema to the great houses. The only innovation was the introduction of the camel corps at the very end of the Arsacid era, and this represented doubling-down on an extant warrior class, the cataphract, as opposed to diversifying the tactical options available. Unlike their Achaemenid predecessors or Sasanian successors, the Parthians do not appear to have utilized elephants for battle. Parthian infantry remained marginal and only suitable for secondary defensive roles throughout the lifetime of the empire. Nor did the Parthians develop a functional capacity for offensive siege warfare. Their only successes in positional warfare occurred as a corollary of driving an already routed Roman force into a town or city that was unprepared for a siege; for example, Crassus at Carrhae in 53 BC and Paetus at Rhandeia in AD 62. In both instances, the Parthians did not even attempt to storm the Roman defences; having lost the will to fight the Romans either broke out in a bid to reach friendly territory or withdrew on terms.

Only with the rise of the successor Sasanian dynasty was Rome confronted with an effectively consolidated rival Persian state. The Sasanians imposed centralized authority far more ruthlessly – and effectively – than the Parthians ever dared. The new rival was not afraid to broaden its military base by adopting a combined-arms approach that incorporated everything from an expanded role for infantry to an elephant corps and a siege train. With a broader fiscal base enabling more efficient administrative infrastructure and logistics, the Sasanians were able to initiate and sustain intensive offensive operations on a scale quite beyond the Parthians. For the first time, the Romans were no longer able to regroup in safety by withdrawing into fortified cities – a fact the Sasanians emphasized by taking Antioch in AD 256. Even the emperors were now at risk on campaign; something Valerian discovered to his cost when he was defeated and captured by the Shah Shapur I in AD 260.

Vologases VI, the last king of the Parthian dynasty, succeeded to the throne in AD 208, but his reign was problematic and ultimately a failure. Locked in a dynastic struggle with his brother, Artabanus V, his control over the Parthian Empire was marginal, and he disappears from history in AD 228 during the reign of Ardashir I (r. AD 224–242), founder of the Sasanian dynasty. (Noble Numismatics, https://www. noble.com.au/)

Conclusion

In the end, Rome might be said to have 'won' its confrontation with Parthia, but ultimately lost by doing so. Although Roman armies had defeated Parthia and repeatedly sacked the Parthian capital, these triumphs were as fleeting as they were expensive. The monarchs of the Arsacid line were always outsiders to the peoples they ruled; their authority relied almost exclusively on prestige which, being eroded by constant humiliation at the hands of Rome, only accelerated the rise of an indigenous Persian reaction that culminated in the succession of the Sasanian dynasty. Rome's only prize for its 'victory' in eliminating an easily contained threat, therefore, was confrontation with a far more dangerous strategic rival. This was the ultimate legacy of what happened on 9 June 53 BC on a dusty plain outside the town of Carrhae. For nearly 700 years, the Fertile Crescent would be divided in half, between a Roman west (modern-day Jordan, Israel, Lebanon, Syria and Turkey) and a Persian east (modern-day Kuwait, Iraq, Iran and Azerbaijan). Armenia would always be contested, and the frontiers would shift incrementally after each war, but always the basic contours would remain the same, until the Arabs, united by the faith of Islam, would sweep the chessboard in the 7th century AD and start a whole new game.

Nothing remains of Ctesiphon, the capital city of the Parthian Empire, beyond the Taq Kasra, the remnant of the Sasanian royal palace. The great arch, 35m high, 25m wide and 46m deep, was until the construction of the Gateway Arch in St. Louis, Missouri, United States, the largest unsupported parabolic arch in the world, and is still the widest span of unsupported brick. The Romans sacked Ctesiphon five times over the course of their forever war with the Persians – in AD 116, 164, 197, 283 and 299. The city lost status after the Arab conquest of the 7th century AD and was abandoned by the end of the 8th century. (Library of Congress)

BIBLIOGRAPHY

Ancient sources

Sextus Julius Africanus (*c*.AD 160–*c*.240) was one of the first Christian historians of Rome. His *Chronographiai*, a history of the world in five volumes from the Creation to the year AD 221, has not survived, but it lives on in the *Chronicon* of Eusebius and the fragments in George Syncellus, Cedrenus and the *Chronicon Paschale* (translated by William Adler, De Gruyter, Berlin, 2012).

Appian (*c*.AD 95–*c*.165) was born in Alexandria but moved to Rome in his adulthood to pursue a legal career. Written in 24 books, his *Roman History* chronicles, explains and justifies Rome's imperial expansion up to the early 2nd century AD.

The Roman statesman, orator, lawyer and philosopher **Marcus Tullius Cicero** (106–43 BC), who was elected consul for the year 63 BC, served as proconsul of Cilicia from May 51 BC to November 50 BC, helping to keep that province in line in the aftermath of the Roman disaster at Carrhae. His letters to his friends and family (translated in four volumes by Evelyn S. Shuckburgh, George Bell & Sons, London, 1905) and *Brutus* (translated by G.L. Hendrickson for Loeb's Classical Library, 1939) offer a fascinating insight into the political machinations of the late republic.

Cassius Dio (*c*.AD 164–after 229), born and raised in Nicaea in Bithynia, served a long and distinguished career holding multiple political offices in addition to authoring his 80-volume *History* of Rome from its founding until AD 229 (translated in nine volumes, 1914–27, by Earnest Cary for Loeb's Classical Library). Much of the text is lost, only surviving in an abridgement by the Byzantine historian Joannes Zonaras. Dio was a senator, the governor of Smyrna, proconsul in Africa and Pannonia, and served as consul twice. His experience in office allows for an intimate understanding of the workings of Roman politics, but also colours his historical narrative; his account of the reign of Caracalla (r. AD 198–217) is invaluable for its detail, but is heavily biased against the emperor.

There are sparse references to the geography and history of Parthia in three comprehensive studies of Rome's world: the *Historical Library* of **Diodorus Siculus** in the 1st century BC (translated in 12 volumes for Loeb's Classical Library, Volume IX by Russel M. Geer, 1947); the *Natural History* of **Pliny the Elder** in the 1st century AD; and the *Geographica* of **Strabo** (64/63 BC–*c*.AD 24) that straddled those eras (available online at http://perseus. uchicago.edu/perseus-cgi/citequery3.pl?dbname=GreekFeb 2011&query=Str.&getid=2).

Three more historians who help flesh out the chronology of Rome are: **Festus** (4th century AD), author of the *Summary of the History of Rome* (available online at http://www.attalus.org/translate/festus.html); **Florus** (1st–2nd century AD), author of *The Two Books of the Epitome, Extracted from Titus Livius, of all the Wars of Seven Hundred Years* (available online at http://penelope.uchicago.edu/ Thayer/E/Roman/Texts/Florus/Epitome/home.html); and **Frontinus** (*c*.AD 40–103), a prominent statesman, serving

The Roman statesman, scholar and writer Marcus Tullius Cicero was no warrior, but the fact that he served as proconsul of Cilicia from May 51 BC to November 50 BC, in the unsettled aftermath of the disaster at Carrhae, gave him uncomfortably close proximity to the ensuing Parthian counter-invasion of Syria. It is thanks to Cicero that we know much about the politics and personalities of his era; for example, Publius Crassus, who fell at Carrhae. Publius had served under Julius Caesar in Gaul, where in 57–56 BC he distinguished himself as a legionary commander in Aquitania. As he made clear in his correspondence with Caesar, Cicero held Publius in high regard, his esteem reinforced by Caesar's similarly positive opinion (Shuckburgh 1905: IV.294). Distinguished by his background and training, Publius embodied many Roman virtues (Hendrickson 1939: 245). (DEA/G. DAGLI ORTI/De Agostini via Getty Images)

as consul three times and as proconsul of Asia in AD 86, and a successful general under Domitian, commanding forces in Britain and on the Rhine and Danube frontiers. This experience informed Frontinus' treatise *The Stratagems*, which offers lessons in military science based on a series of case studies from Rome's record on the battlefield.

A novel of the 3rd or 4th century AD, the *Aethiopica* by **Heliodorus of Emesa** (translated by Moses Hadas, University of Michigan Press, Ann Arbor, MI, 1957) contains detailed descriptions of cataphract arms and armour, as does the 4th-century AD chronicler **Ammianus Marcellinus** in his *History, Vol. II: Books 20–26* (translated for Loeb's Classical Library by J. C. Rolfe, 1940) and the rhetorician and panegyrist **Nazarius** in an AD 321 speech delivered to celebrate the 15th anniversary of the accession of Constantine the Great (r. AD 306–37).

Herodian (*c*.AD 170–*c*.240), was a minor Roman civil servant whose eight-volume *History of the Empire from the Death of Marcus* (available online at https://www.livius.org/sources/content/herodian-s-roman-history/) covers the years AD 180–238. Alongside Dio, his account is the most complete on the Parthian campaign of Caracalla.

Titus Flavius Josephus (AD 37–100), born Yosef ben Matityahu, was a fighter in the Judean Revolt that broke out in AD 66 who defected to Rome. His works *The Jewish War* and *Antiquities of the Jews* (translated by William Whiston and published by John E. Potter, Philadelphia, PA, 1895) focus on the history of his people, but provide useful anecdotes on the ill-fated campaign of Crassus and the Parthian interventions under Pacorus in the wake of Carrhae and Philippi.

The life of **Marcus Junianus Justinus** is lost to history, his contribution to history being the *Epitome of the Philippic History of Pompeius Trogus* (translated by John Selby Watson, Bohn, London, 1853) which summarizes the work of that 1st-century BC historian,

providing very useful details on the origins, rise and customs of the Parthians.

The poetry of **Lucan** (AD 39–65) is grounded in the reality of his era, making his *Pharsalia* (translated by Sir Edward Ridley, Longmans, London, 1905) replete with keen insights into personalities, politics and the tactics and technology of battle.

The *Compendium of Roman History* of **Marcus Velleius Paterculus** (*c*.19 BC–*c*.AD 31) covers the period from the end of the Trojan War to the death of Livia in AD 29 (translated by Frederick W. Shipley for Loeb Classical Library, 1924). Paterculus served as military tribune in Thrace, Macedonia, Greece and the East, and in AD 2 was present at the conference on the Euphrates between Gaius Caesar, grandson of Augustus, and the Parthian king Phraates IV. He subsequently served for eight years in Germany and Pannonia under Tiberius. He was elected quaestor in AD 8, and praetor in AD 15.

Plutarch (*c*.AD 46–*c*.120) was born to a prominent Greek family in the small town of Chaeronea. Having received his education at the Academy in Athens, for many years Plutarch served as one of the two priests at the temple of Apollo at Delphi, the site of the famous Oracle. His *Parallel Lives* (translated by A.H. Clough, Little, Brown & Co., Boston, MA, 1876) intended to draw moral lessons by comparing and contrasting Greek and Roman statesmen, includes invaluable chapters on Crassus and Antony.

The *Annals* and *Histories* (translated by Moses Hadas, Modern Library, New York, NY, 2003) of **Tacitus** (*c*.AD 56–*c*.120) offer a critical insight into the reigns of the successors to Augustus.

Writing in the late empire, **Vegetius** (4th–5th centuries AD) offered in his *De re militari* (translated by John Clarke, W. Griffin, London, 1767) a textbook guide to military organization that harkens back to the triumphs of an earlier era.

Secondary sources

Anderson, Erich B. (2016). *Cataphracts: Knights of the Ancient Eastern Empires*. Barnsley: Pen & Sword.

Bennett, Julian (2006). *Trajan, Optimus Princeps: A Life and Times*. New York, NY: Routledge.

Campbell, Duncan B. (1986). 'What Happened at Hatra? The Problem of the Severan Siege', in Philip W. Freeman and David L. Kennedy, eds, *The Defence of the Roman and Byzantine East: Proceedings of a Colloquium held at the University of Sheffield*, BAR International Series, No. 297: pp. 51–58.

Coulston, J.C.N. (1986). 'Roman, Parthian and Sassanid Tactical Developments', in Philip W. Freeman and David L. Kennedy, eds, *The Defence of the Roman and Byzantine East: Proceedings of a Colloquium held at the University of Sheffield*, BAR International Series, No. 297: pp. 59–75.

Cowan, Ross (2003a). *Roman Legionary 58 BC–AD 69*. Warrior 71. Oxford: Osprey.

Cowan, Ross (2003b). *Imperial Roman Legionary AD 161–284*. Warrior 72. Oxford: Osprey.

Cowan, Ross (2009). 'The Battle of Nisibis, AD 217', *Ancient Warfare*, Vol. III, No. 5: 29–35.

Cowan, Ross (2013). *Roman Legionary AD 69–161*. Warrior 166. Oxford: Osprey.

Cowan, Ross (2015). *Imperial Roman Legionary AD 284–337*. Warrior 175. Oxford: Osprey.

Curtis, Vesta S. & Stewart, Sarah (2010). *The Age of the Parthians*. London: I.B. Tauris & Co.

Debevoise, Neilson C. (1938). *A Political History of Parthia*. Chicago, IL: University of Chicago Press.

Farrokh, Kaveh (2009). *Shadows in the Desert: Ancient Persia at War*. Oxford: Osprey.

Ferguson, R. James (2005). 'Rome and Parthia: Power Politics and Diplomacy Across Cultural Frontiers', in *The Centre for East–West Cultural and Economic Studies*, Research Paper No. 12. Available at http://epublications.bond.edu.au/cgi/viewcontent.cgi?article=1009&context=cewces_papers

Goldsworthy, Adrian (2003). *In the Name of Rome: The Men Who Won the Roman Empire*. London: Weidenfeld & Nicolson.

Goldsworthy, Adrian (2009). *The Roman Army at War, 100 BC–AD 200*. Oxford: Clarendon Press.

Hanson, Victor D. (2002). *Carnage and Culture: Landmark Battles in the Rise of Western Power*. New York, NY: Anchor.

Harl, Kenneth W. (2016). 'Rome's Greatest Foe: Rome versus Parthia and Sassanid Persia', Chapter 3, in James Lacey, ed., *Great Strategic Rivalries: From the Classical World to the Cold War*, Oxford & New York, NY: Oxford University Press: pp. 102–153.

James, Simon (2009). *The Excavations at Dura-Europos conducted by Yale University and the French Academy of Inscriptions and Letters 1928 to 1937. Final Report VII: The Arms and Armour and other Military Equipment*. Havertown, PA: Oxbow.

Keaveney, Arthur (1982). 'The King and the War-Lords: Romano-Parthian Relations Circa 64–53 B.C.', *The American Journal of Philology*, Vol. 103, No. 4: 412–428.

Lightfoot, C.S. (1990). 'Trajan's Parthian War and the Fourth-Century Perspective', *The Journal of Roman Studies*, Vol. 80: 115–126.

Loades, Mike (2016). *The Composite Bow*. Weapon 43. Oxford: Osprey.

Mattern-Parkes, Susan P. (2003). 'The Defeat of Crassus and the Just War', *The Classical World*, Vol. 96, No. 4: 387–396.

Mielczarek, Mariusz (1993). *Cataphracti and Clibanarii: Studies on the Heavy Armoured Cavalry of the Ancient World*. Łódź: Oficyna Naukowa MS.

Ratzel, Friedrich (1896). 'The Territorial Growth of States', *The Scottish Geographical Magazine*, Vol. XII, No. 1: 351–361.

Rea, Cam (2014). *Leviathan vs. Behemoth: The Roman-Parthian Wars 66 BC–217 AD*. Online Platform, CreateSpace.

Sampson, Gareth C. (2015). *The Defeat of Rome: Crassus, Carrhae and the Invasion of the East*. Barnsley: Pen & Sword.

Seaver, James E. (1952). 'Publius Ventidius: Neglected Roman Military Hero', *The Classical Journal*, Vol. 47, No. 7: 275–280.

Sheldon, Rose M. (2010). *Rome's Wars in Parthia*. London: Vallentine Mitchell.

Sicker, Martin (2000). *The Pre-Islamic Middle East*. Westport, CT: Praeger.

Strugnell, Emma (2006). 'Ventidius' Parthian War: Rome's Forgotten Eastern Triumph', *Acta Antiqua Academiae Scientiarum Hungaricae*, No. 46: 239–252.

Syvänne, Ilkka (2017). 'Parthian Cataphract vs. the Roman Army, 53 BC–AD 224', *Historia I Świat*, No. 6: 33–54.

Syvänne, Ilkka (2017). *Caracalla: A Military Biography*. Barnsley: Pen & Sword.

Traina, Giusto (2011). 'Imperial Views on the Battle of Carrhae', in Hartmut Böhme and Marco Formisano, eds, *War in Words: Transformations of War from Antiquity to Clausewitz*, Berlin: De Gruyter: pp. 209–217.

Ward, Allen M. (1977). *Marcus Crassus and the Late Roman Republic*. Columbia, MO: University of Missouri Press.

Warry, John (1995). *Warfare in the Classical World*. Norman, OK: University of Oklahoma Press.

Wheeler, Everett L. (1997). 'Why the Romans can't defeat the Parthians: Julius Africanus and the Strategy of Magic', in W. Groenman-van Waateringe, ed., *Roman Frontier Studies 1995*, Oxford: Oxbow: pp. 575–579.

Wilcox, Peter (1986). *Rome's Enemies (3): Parthians & Sassanid Persians*. Men-at-Arms 175. Oxford: Osprey.

Woźniak, Marek A. (2019). *Armies of Ancient Persia: From the Founding of the Achaemenid State to the Fall of the Sassanid Empire*. Lawrence, KS: Winged Hussar Publishing.

Wroth, Warwick (1903). *A Catalogue of the Greek Coins in the British Museum: Catalogue of the Coins of Parthia*. London: Longman's.

Wylie, G.J. (1993). 'P. Ventidius – From Novus Homo to "Military Hero"', *Acta Classica*, Vol. XXXVI: 129–141.

Yu, Taishan (1998). 'A Study of Saka History', *Sino-Platonic Papers*, No. 80: 1–225.

INDEX